From our Kitchen to Yours

Quick & Easy Recipes
with Help...

FROM MY INSTANT POT®, AIR FRYER, SLOW COOKER, WAFFLE IRON & MORE

Dedication

For every cook who enjoys using their favorite appliances and bake ware to make delicious and easy meals for their family & friends.

•••••••••••••••••••••••

Appreciation

Thanks to everyone who shared their delightful and tasty recipes with us!

•••••••••••••••••••••••

Gooseberry Patch
An imprint of Globe Pequot
246 Goose Lane • Guilford, CT 06437

www.gooseberrypatch.com
1•800•854•6673

Copyright © 2022, Gooseberry Patch
978-1-62093-477-7

Welcome

Dear Friends,
Quick & Easy Recipes with Help from my Instant Pot®, Air Fryer, Slow Cooker, Waffle Iron & More *is the perfect cookbook to help you get the most from your kitchen appliances and bake ware. With recipes geared to your favorite kitchen helpers, you'll make these yummy dishes again and again. Air Fryer recipes like Roasted Butternut Squash (page 18) and Crispy Potato Chips (page 12) are sure to become a hit...and you can make them in a matter of minutes. Chicago Italian Beef (page 36), made in your Instant Pot, is so tender and delicious...they will be asking for seconds! You'll love the Slow-Cooker Country Chicken & Dumplings (page 88) and Slow-Cooker Swiss Steak (page 98) for those special comfort-food meals. Your tried & true blender can whip up Strawberry Preserves Smoothies (page 138) or Butternut Squash Soup (page 142) in no time. Need a clever dessert? Try our Chocolate Waffle Ice Cream Treats (page 166) for a sweet surprise they are sure to love. Love those one-pan meals? Then pull out your sheet pan to make Baked Chicken Chimichangas (page 198) or some Good and "Healthy" Fried Chicken (page 194). That trusty cast-iron skillet is just waiting to cook Grilled Havarti Sandwiches (page 236) and your muffin tin is perfect for Mini Ham & Swiss Frittatas (page 258). We are so pleased to bring you this cookbook filled with quick & easy recipes that offers dozens of fresh, fun and satisfying recipes that you can make with a little assistance from your favorite kitchen helpers. Enjoy!*

Sincerely,
Jo Ann & Vickie

Table of Contents

Introduction

Kitchen Helpers

As we begin to cook a meal for our family or friends, we may take for granted some of the kitchen helpers that make cooking easier and more efficient. It might be that trusty **Slow Cooker** that you have had for years that steps up every time you have a busy schedule and need to be gone for the day. That shiny new **Instant Pot®** or **Air Fryer** that you have learned to love is ready for action to make your meal in a jiffy, almost like magic. Your **Waffle Iron** might be almost vintage by now, but you reach for it every time you want a quick breakfast or dinner that you know everyone will love. The seasoned **Cast-Iron Skillet** is a heavy-duty worker that you can count on for comforting meals. Your **Blender** has served you well for years and you return to it again and again for last-minute recipes that whip up in no time. And don't forget those **Sheet Pans** and **Muffin Tins** that are always there just when you need them for a one-pan dinner or tasty individual treats. Make the most of these kitchen helpers with recipes that will please your family & friends.

Instant Pot®

While this appliance may be a relatively new member of your appliance team, the electric pressure cooker could be considered one of the new stars. Some of us may remember the pressure cooker that our mother or grandmother used. It was a large, heavy metal pan with a jiggling top that demanded respect and attention while it cooked on the stovetop. Today's version of this kitchen appliance is quite different. It is a multi-functional cooker that allows the cook to prepare a meal in a fraction of the time while keeping more nutrients in the food from cooking away. It prepares tasty one-pot meals in minutes, sautés and then cooks meat deliciously, prepares hard-cooked eggs that are easy to peel and makes creamy yogurt. The brand that is one of the most common is the Instant Pot®. In many recipes and books the electric pressure cooker and Instant Pot® names are used interchangeably. The information we give here refers to most electric pressure cookers and primarily the Instant Pot® brand. Here are some tips for using your electric pressure cooker:

1. **Cool Before Opening** Never open the electric pressure cooker until the cooker has cooled and all internal pressure has been released. If the float valve is still up or the lid is difficult to turn, it is an indication that the cooker is still pressurized. Never force it open. Simply wait until the float valve is down.

2. **Release Valve** Make sure the steam release valve is in the Sealing position for all the pressure-cooking programs. This is the only way that the pressure can build in the cooker.

3. **Space for Pressure** For all pressure-cooking programs, the total amount of precooked food and liquid in the inner pot should not pass the 2/3 line. When cooking food that expands during cooking such as rice, beans or vegetables, the inner pot should not pass the 1/2 line. This is because there needs to be enough space for the pressure to build.

4. **Don't Overfill** Electric pressure cookers come in various sizes. For most recipes, the 6 or 8-quart size will work. If you are using a smaller pot, be sure that the amount of precooked food does not exceed the line in the pot for maximum amount.

5. **Be Aware** Certain foods, such as applesauce, cranberries, rhubarb, split peas, pearl barley, oatmeal and other cereals, noodles and pasta can foam, froth, sputter, and clog the steam release. Be sure you watch your cooker carefully and press Cancel if it seems that the pressure is not releasing as it should.

6. **Use Oven Mitts** Always use oven mitts when removing the inner pot after cooking or releasing any remaining pressure. Steam is very hot and can burn very quickly. Never put your face or hands over the steam valve to check it.

7. **Always Read Manufacturer's Instructions** Different brands of cookers can vary. Be familiar with the brand you choose.

Air Fryer

The air fryer is a handy appliance that is really a version of a countertop convection oven. It acts like it fries the food but it uses hot air to cook with little or no oil, making the food crispy and not oily. It is great for quick-cooking foods like French fries, vegetables, frozen foods and even cookies. The top section of an air fryer holds a heating device with a fan. You place the food in a fryer-style basket, turn it on and the air flows around the food. This fast circulation makes the food crisp, but without the oil. These are the simple steps for air frying:

1. Set the time and temperature on the fryer as instructed in the recipe.

2. Spray the basket with non-stick vegetable spray if the recipe tells you to. When prompted, place the food in the basket.

3. Cook the food. You may need to turn the food or shake the basket. Most recipes are done in 5 to 20 minutes, making the air fryer a convenient way to prepare a snack or meal.

Introduction

Sheet Pans and Skillets

You may have had sheet pans and skillets in your cupboard for years, but until now you may not have realized just how amazing they are! That sheet pan that you thought was only for dessert bars can cook a pork chop dinner in no time. And the ho-hum skillet you have reserved for frying an egg can make an amazing pizza or dessert. The best part of all...these humble pans can save you so much time and energy when it comes to clean-up! Sheet pans are a must in your kitchen. They are hard-working, affordable, durable and easy to clean. They conduct heat quickly and because they have a low edge, they allow the heat to circulate well and come in contact with more surface area on the food. The pan is large enough to allow you to spread out the meat or veggies without crowding. The name "sheet pan" can be a bit confusing. A sheet pan has a rimmed edge all the way around and is a type of baking sheet. Most cooks use the terms sheet pan and baking sheet interchangeably. The typical sheet pan is a heavy-duty, usually aluminum, pan measuring about 18x13 inches or sometimes 15x10 inches with a rim all the way around that is about an inch tall.

Skillets are rough-and-ready pans that can be made from cast iron, stainless steel, copper or combinations of metals that transfer heat well. Choose a skillet that is easy for you to handle and make sure you have at least one that can go into the oven as well as on the stovetop. Cast-iron skillets are known for their heat retention and even heating and they stay warm longer than other metal types. You can bake or roast in a cast-iron skillet as well. Some skillets have a non-stick surface which comes in handy for many recipes.

Slow Cooker

Cooking pots that resembled the slow cooker of today actually began about 80 years ago. But it was in 1971 that the version of the slow cooker that we know today became available on the market. Cooks fell in love with the ease of cooking that it provided. The "fix it and forget it" concept of a slow cooker was just too good to be true. Ingredients were all tossed into the cooker in the morning, and by dinnertime a meal was ready for the family. Today, more sophisticated recipes and cookers make this tried & true appliance even more popular with cooks everywhere.

Waffle Irons and Waffle Makers

Waffle irons have been around for a long time. Vintage styles can still be found that consist of two iron plates with wooden handles designed to be used on an open fire. The ones we enjoy today are electric and come in all shapes and sizes. One of the most popular is the Belgian-style waffle makers that produces deeper-pocket waffles that hold plenty of syrup. There are also individual waffle makers, waffle makers with grids that produce images, heart-shaped styles and more. Filled with ice cream or fruit, covered in syrup, or served with fried chicken, everyone loves waffles.

Muffin Tin

A muffin tin or muffin cup tray is a mold that is usually used to bake muffins or cupcakes. Most molds have individual cups for 12 muffins, although tins holding 6, 8, and 24 muffins are also available. Muffin tins can be made from aluminum, enamel, cast iron or silicone. Some have non-stick coatings. Because the pan makes individual servings, it is also convenient to use for appetizers and main-dish recipes such as egg and vegetable dishes.

Blender

The ever-ready blender is a staple in most kitchens. Primarily used for mixing drinks, this convenient appliance is also a must for soups, sauces and dips. A welcome appliance for making smoothies in the morning, it is also equally as useful for pureeing or blending ingredients for lunch or dinner. The immersion blender, a cousin to the traditional stand model, is especially helpful for blending right in the same cooking pot. This seemingly old-fashioned appliance is anything but dated when it comes to helping out in the kitchen.

CHAPTER 1

Air Fryer Recipes

Whether you are just getting to know your air fryer as a new appliance in your kitchen or if you are an old hand at preparing meals in this convenient appliance, you'll love the wide range of recipes that you can fix for snacking and dining. In this chapter featuring the air fryer, you'll find everything from savory Roasted Butternut Squash and Quick Cheesy Sticks to sweet Mini Cinnobuns and Gram's Zucchini Cookies. Your air fryer is so handy for cooking snacks like Personal Pizzas and Crispy Potato Chips when you need something for the kids in just a few minutes. And mealtime is more fun when clean-up is easy! So get ready to enjoy cooking in your air fryer with recipes that cut the time you spend in the kitchen...giving you more time to share delicious dishes with family & friends.

Cindy Atkins, *Vancouver, WA*

Creamy Tuna Melts

These get so crispy and yummy in the air fryer. This is one of our favorite Sunday night suppers.

Serves 8

2 to 3 stalks celery, diced
1 onion, diced
12-oz. can tuna, drained
½ c. cottage cheese
½ c. mayonnaise
¼ t. garlic salt
⅛ t. sugar
4 English muffins, split and toasted
8 slices American cheese

Spray the air fryer basket with non-stick vegetable spray. In a skillet, sauté celery and onion until tender. Add tuna, cottage cheese, mayonnaise, garlic salt and sugar to skillet. Mix well, breaking up tuna. Cook over low heat until warmed through, stirring frequently; remove from heat. Place muffins cut-side down in basket. Cook for 3 minutes. Remove muffins and flip over. Spread with tuna mixture; top with cheese slices. Working in batches, cook in air fryer until cheese melts, about 4 minutes. Serve immediately.

Lyne Neymeyer, *Des Moines, IA*

Olive & Sausage Meatballs

You'll love the surprise flavor of black and green olives in these appetizer-size meatballs.

Makes about 2 dozen

1 egg, beaten
1 T. green olives, diced
1 T. black olives, diced
½ c. dry bread crumbs
1 T. fresh parsley, minced
1 lb. ground pork sausage
1 lb. lean ground beef
1 T. grated Parmesan cheese
Optional: pretzel sticks

Preheat air fryer to 400 degrees. Spray basket with non-stick vegetable spray. In a bowl, combine egg, olives, bread crumbs and parsley. Add sausage, ground beef and cheese; mix well. Shape into 1¼-inch balls. Place in a single layer in air fryer basket. Working in batches, cook for about 10 minutes until lightly browned and meat thermometer reaches 160 degrees. Remove and keep warm; repeat with remaining meatballs. If desired, insert a pretzel stick in each meatball.

Olive & Sausage Meatballs

Kathy Wood, *La Crescenta, CA*

Crispy Chicken Fingers

Everyone thinks these are a treat for a quick lunch or late evening meal.

Serves 6

¾ c. Italian-flavored dry bread crumbs
1 T. grated Parmesan cheese
¼ t. garlic, minced
¼ c. buttermilk
3 boneless, skinless chicken breasts

Spray air fryer basket with non-stick vegetable spray. Preheat air fryer to 375 degrees. Combine bread crumbs and cheese in a shallow dish; set aside. Combine garlic and buttermilk in a small bowl; set aside. Place chicken between 2 sheets of heavy-duty plastic wrap. Flatten chicken to ½-inch thickness, using a meat mallet or rolling pin; cut into one-inch-wide strips. Dip strips in buttermilk mixture; coat with crumb mixture. Working in batches, cook for about 15 minutes, turning after 10 minutes, until golden brown and meat thermometer reads 165 degrees.

Judy Bailey, *Des Moines, Iowa*

Crispy Potato Chips

My husband Denny and I make these for a snack in the evenings. They always turn out great!

Serves 4

3 6-oz. russet potatoes, cut into ⅛-inch slices
1 T. canola oil
¼ t. sea salt
¼ t. pepper

Place sliced potatoes in a large bowl of cold water for 30 minutes; drain and pat dry. Place potatoes into a shallow bowl and add oil, salt and pepper; toss to coat. Lightly coat air-fryer basket with non-stick vegetable spray. Preheat air fryer to 375 degrees. Working in batches, place potatoes in prepared basket. Cook 15 to 20 minutes or until crisp. Using tongs, transfer chips to a plate. Repeat with remaining potatoes. Sprinkle with more salt if desired.

Crispy Potato Chips

Tori Willis, *Champaign, IL*

Minted Baby Carrots

I make these carrots often...they are so easy to fix in the air fryer and go with any meat I serve.

Serves 4

½ lb. baby carrots
1 T. butter, melted
salt and pepper to taste
1 T. lemon zest, minced
1 T. brown sugar, packed
2 T. fresh mint, minced

Place carrots in large bowl. Combine butter, salt and pepper, lemon zest and brown sugar in small bowl. Pour over carrots: toss well. Preheat air fryer to 390 degrees. Cook 6 to 8 minutes, shaking occasionally during cooking, until carrots are tender and lightly browned. Remove to serving dish. Sprinkle with fresh mint.

Carol Field Dahlstrom, *Ankeny, IA*

Personal Pizzas

Let the kids pick their own toppings!

Makes 4 pizzas

4 t. olive oil, divided
½ c. pizza sauce, divided
6-oz. pkg. sliced pepperoni, divided
1 c. shredded mozzarella cheese, divided
1 t. crushed red pepper flakes
½ t. salt
Garnish: fresh arugula

Preheat air fryer to 375 degrees. Divide prepared Pizza Dough into four 4 portions. On a lightly floured surface, roll one portion of dough into a 7-inch circle. Make holes in the crust with a fork. Place in air-fryer basket and cook 3 minutes. Remove from basket, flip over onto work surface. Drizzle crust with one teaspoon of oil and spread with 2 tablespoons pizza sauce. Place pepperoni on top; sprinkle with ¼ cup mozzarella cheese, ¼ teaspoon red pepper flakes and ⅛ teaspoon salt. Return pizza to air-fryer basket and cook 5 to 6 minutes or until cheese is melted and golden. Top with fresh arugula and serve. Repeat with remaining dough and toppings.

PIZZA DOUGH:

1 env. active dry yeast
⅔ c. warm water, 110 to 115 degrees
1 t. sugar
½ t. salt
1 T. olive oil
2 c. all-purpose flour

Sprinkle yeast into water. Let set for 10 minutes. Add sugar, salt and oil; stir. Add flour. Turn out on board and knead until elastic. Cover and let rise for 20 minutes.

Personal Pizzas

Carol Hickman, *Kingsport, TN*

Salmon Patties

A delicious standby...so quick to fix, and most of the ingredients are right in the cupboard.

Serves 5 to 6

15½-oz. can salmon, drained and flaked
½ c. round buttery crackers, crushed
½ T. dried parsley
½ t. lemon zest
1 T. lemon juice
2 green onions, sliced
1 egg, beaten

Combine all ingredients and mix well; form into 5 to 6 patties. Set aside. Lightly coat air-fryer basket with non-stick vegetable spray. Preheat air fryer to 375 degrees. Working in batches, place patties in prepared basket. Cook 15 to 20 minutes or until golden, turning at least once. Using tongs, transfer to a plate. Serve with Cucumber Sauce.

CUCUMBER SAUCE:

⅓ c. cucumber, chopped
¼ c. plain yogurt
¼ c. mayonnaise
¼ t. dried tarragon

Combine all ingredients; chill until ready to serve

Elijah Dahlstrom, *Ames, IA*

Brussels Sprouts & Bacon

My Dad and I like Brussels sprouts but my sister doesn't like them very much. So Dad and I cook just a few in the air fryer with bacon. We love this recipe.

Makes 4 servings

2 c. Brussels sprouts, trimmed and cut in
    half lengthwise
4 slices bacon, cut into ½-inch pieces
3 t. brown sugar, packed
¼ t. salt
¼ t. pepper

Combine Brussels sprouts, bacon and brown sugar in large bowl. Coat air-fryer basket with non-stick vegetable spray. Preheat air fryer to 370 degrees. Cook about 8 minutes, shaking occasionally during cooking, until slightly charred. Season with salt and pepper.

Brussels Sprouts & Bacon

Mary Bruhn, *Newton, IA*

Crispy Tortilla Chips

These sweet treats are so easy to make!

Serves 4

2 flour tortillas
2 whole-grain tortillas
1 T. canola oil
¼ t. sea salt
Optional: favorite pesto sauce

Cut tortillas into small wedges. Place in shallow bowl and toss with oil. Lightly coat air-fryer basket with non-stick vegetable spray. Preheat air fryer to 375 degrees. Working in batches, place tortillas in prepared basket. Cook 10 to 15 minutes or until crisp. Using tongs, transfer chips to a plate. Repeat with remaining pieces. Sprinkle with salt. Serve with pesto sauce if desired.

Allison May, *Seattle, WA*

Roasted Butternut Squash

This is my go-to vegetable for the entire family...the bite-size pieces make it easy and fun to eat!

Makes 6 servings

2-lb. butternut squash, peeled, seeded and cut into 1-inch pieces
1 T. olive oil
½ t. salt
½ t. pepper
2 T. crumbled Cotija or mozzarella cheese
2 T. toasted pumpkin seeds (pepitas)

Spray the air fryer basket with non-stick vegetable spray. Preheat air fryer to 400 degrees. In a medium bowl, toss together squash, oil, salt and pepper. Working in batches, place squash in a single layer in prepared basket. Cook 10 to 15 minutes or until squash is tender and begins to brown, stirring or shaking basket. Transfer squash to a serving bowl. Sprinkle with cheese and pumpkin seeds.

Roasted Butternut Squash

Marion Sundberg, *Ramona, CA*

Parmesan Zucchini Sticks

Serve these tasty zucchini sticks instead of French fries alongside cheeseburgers...kids will gobble them up!

Serves 4

1 egg
½ c. Italian-flavored dry bread crumbs
½ c. grated Parmesan cheese
1 t. dried thyme
½ t. pepper
6 small zucchini, quartered lengthwise
Garnish: ranch salad dressing

Spray air fryer basket with non-stick vegetable spray. Preheat air fryer to 370 degrees. Place egg in a shallow bowl and beat well; set aside. Mix bread crumbs, cheese, thyme and pepper in a separate bowl. Dip zucchini into egg mixture, letting excess drip back into bowl. Roll in bread crumb mixture to coat. Cook in batches 10 to 12 minutes, shaking halfway through cooking, until golden. Serve with ranch dressing.

Andrew Neymeyer, *Des Moines, IA*

Pepperoni Pizza Sandwiches

These are my go-to sandwiches after work when there are school activities that evening. Quick, easy and delicious!

Serves 6

3 bagels, halved
½ c. pizza sauce, divided
8-oz. pkg. shredded Italian-style cheese, divided
5-oz. pkg. mini pepperoni slices

Preheat air fryer to 360 degrees. Spray air fryer basket with non-stick vegetable spray. Lay bagels with cut side down and cook for 3 minutes. Remove and flip over on work surface. Spread a thin layer of sauce on each bagel. Sprinkle a layer of cheese on the sauce. Top with slices of pepperoni. Top with more cheese, if desired. Cook for about 10 minutes, until cheese is melted. Serve immediately.

Pepperoni Pizza Sandwiches

Jodi Eisenhooth, *McVeytown, PA*

Pecan Cookie Balls

Make these sweet, crisp little morsels to go with an after-dinner cup of tea or coffee.

Makes 2 ½ to 3 dozen

1 c. butter, softened
1 ¼ c. powdered sugar, divided
2 c. chopped pecans
1 T. vanilla extract
2 c. all-purpose flour

Blend together butter and one cup powdered sugar; add pecans, vanilla and flour. Wrap dough in plastic wrap; chill for about 3 hours. Form dough into ¾-inch balls. Preheat air fryer to 360 degrees. Spray air fryer basket with non-stick vegetable spray. Working in batches, place balls on parchment paper and put in basket. Cook for about 10 to 15 minutes turning once. Let cool; roll in remaining powdered sugar.

Diane Stevenson, *Marion, IA*

Mini Cinnobuns

So sweet to eat yet simple to make, you will be serving these yummy treats again and again.

Makes 2 dozen

2 T. brown sugar, packed
2 t. cinnamon
8-oz. pkg. refrigerated crescent roll dough
1 T. butter, melted
2 T. dried cranberries
1 T. chopped pecans
1 c. powdered sugar
1 to 1½ T. orange juice

Combine brown sugar and cinnamon in a small bowl; mix well and set aside. Unroll dough and separate into two 12-inch by 4-inch rectangles; firmly press perforations to seal. Brush dough with melted butter and sprinkle with brown sugar mixture. Sprinkle with cranberries and pecans. Starting with long side, roll up tightly jelly-roll style; pinch seams to seal. Cut each roll crosswise into 12 one-inch slices with a serrated knife. Preheat air fryer to 370 degrees. Bake in batches for 8 to 10 minutes or until golden. Remove to wire rack; cool. Combine powdered sugar and one tablespoon orange juice in a small bowl; whisk until smooth. Add additional juice, one teaspoon at a time, to reach desired glaze consistency. Drizzle glaze over buns.

Mini Cinnobuns

Diane Axtell, *Marble Falls, TX*

Oh-So-Easy Hot Dogs

If you don't have time to fire up the grill, the air fryer is the perfect appliance to take its place when you want a quick hot dog...and clean up time is a snap.

Serves 8

8 fully-cooked hot dogs
8 hot dog buns, split
Optional: catsup, mustard, pickle relish,
**   onion slices**

Preheat air fryer to 350 degrees. Spray air fryer basket with non-stick vegetable spray. Working in batches, lay 4 hot dogs in the fryer basket. Cook for about 8 minutes, turning once, until hot dogs are sizzling. Turn temperature down to 200 degrees and lay buns on top of hot dogs. Warm for 2 minutes or less. Remove from basket and serve. Repeat with remaining hot dogs.

> **⟿ Kitchen Tip ⟿**
>
> While some air fryer recipes may not mention spraying the air fryer basket with non-stick vegetable spray, it is important in almost all recipes. There is no fat in the air fryer and non-stick vegetable spray adds just a little oil for texture and flavor as well as making clean-up much easier.

Henry Burnley, *Ankeny, IA*

Quick Cheesy Sticks

My grandma and I made these together and I love them. They taste like the ones we get in my favorite restaurant.

Makes 4 servings

¼ c. all-purpose flour
2 eggs
1 T. water
1 c. plain dry bread crumbs
½ t. salt
½ t. pepper
12-oz. pkg. string cheese sticks
1 c. marinara or pizza sauce, warmed

Put flour in a small bowl; set aside. In another small bowl, whisk together eggs and water. Combine bread crumbs, salt and pepper in third small bowl. Coat each piece of cheese with flour. Dip into egg mixture, letting excess drip back into bowl. Roll in bread crumb mixture to coat. Dip again in egg mixture and roll again in bread crumb mixture. Refrigerate or freeze until ready to cook. Spray basket with non-stick vegetable spray. Preheat air fryer to 370 degrees. Cook in batches 6 to 8 minutes, shaking halfway through cooking, until golden and cheese just begins to melt. Serve with marinara or pizza sauce.

Quick Cheesy Sticks

Susanne Erickson, *Columbus, OH*

Chinese Chicken Wings

Move over, hot wings. These Asian-inspired chicken wings are packed with flavor and they're made in the air fryer. Make extra, because the crowd will love them!

Makes 2 to 3 dozen, serves 12

3 lbs. chicken wings
1/2 c. low-sodium soy sauce
1 c. pineapple juice
1/3 c. brown sugar, packed
1 t. ground ginger
1/2 t. pepper
Optional: celery sticks, ranch salad dressing

Place wings in a large plastic zipping bag; set aside. Combine soy sauce, pineapple juice, brown sugar, ginger and pepper; pour over wings, turning to coat. Refrigerate overnight, turning several times. Drain wings, discarding marinade. Preheat air fryer to 425 degrees. Spray the basket with non-stick vegetable spray. Working in batches, arrange the wings in a single layer on the basket. Cook for 25 to 30 minutes, turning once, until golden and juices run clear when chicken is pierced with a fork. Serve with celery and ranch dressing, if desired.

Debi DeVore, *Dover, OH*

Spiced Orange Pecans

A tasty hostess gift that's sure to be welcome...and so easy to make in your air fryer.

Makes about 3 1/2 cups, serves 16

2 egg whites, beaten
3 T. orange juice
2 c. pecan halves
1 c. powdered sugar
2 T. cornstarch
1 T. orange zest
1 t. cinnamon
3/4 t. ground cloves
1/4 t. allspice
1/8 t. salt

Beat egg white and orange juice in medium bowl. Add pecans; stir until well coated. In a separate bowl, combine remaining ingredients. Combine nuts and sugar mixture; toss until well coated. Preheat air fryer to 300 degrees. Spray basket with non-stick vegetable spray. Working in batches, cook 12 to 15 minutes, shaking several times during cooking. Cool slightly. Store in airtight container up to 2 weeks.

Spiced Orange Pecans

Tracey Ten Eyck, *Austin, TX*

Chocolate Chip-Oat Cookies

This recipe was handed down to me by my mother, many years ago. She made the best homemade cookies ever! Now I make a few at a time in my air fryer. So crispy and good.

Makes 4 dozen

1 c. butter
¾ c. brown sugar, packed
¾ c. sugar
2 eggs
1 t. hot water
1½ c. all-purpose flour
1 t. baking soda
1 t. salt
12-oz. pkg. semi-sweet mini chocolate chips
2 c. long-cooking oats, uncooked
Optional: 1 c. nuts, finely chopped
1 t. vanilla extract

In a large bowl, beat butter until soft. Gradually add sugars, blending until light and fluffy. Add eggs, one at a time, beating well after each addition. Stir in hot water. In a separate bowl, mix together flour, baking soda and salt; gradually add flour mixture to butter mixture. Stir in chocolate chips, oats and nuts, if desired; mix thoroughly. Add vanilla extract and blend well. Preheat air fryer to 360 degrees. Working in batches, drop dough by small teaspoonfuls onto parchment paper and place in basket. Cook for 8 to 12 minutes, until golden. Remove to wire racks to cool.

Sharon Levandowski, *Hoosick Falls, NY*

Gram's Zucchini Cookies

Who would think zucchini would make these cookies so yummy? And who would think you can bake them in your air fryer?

Makes 4 dozen

¾ c. butter, softened
1½ c. sugar
1 egg, beaten
1 t. vanilla extract
1½ c. zucchini, grated and well-drained
2½ c. all-purpose flour
2 t. baking powder
1 t. cinnamon
½ t. salt
1 c. chopped walnuts or almonds
6-oz. pkg. semi-sweet mini chocolate chips

Blend together butter and sugar in a bowl; beat in egg and vanilla. Stir in zucchini. In a separate bowl, combine flour, baking powder, cinnamon and salt; gradually add to butter mixture. Stir in nuts and chocolate chips. Heat air fryer to 375 degrees. Working in batches, drop dough by small teaspoonfuls onto parchment paper and place in basket. Cook for 13 to 15 minutes, until golden. Remove to wire racks to cool.

Gram's Zucchini Cookies

Diane Axtell, *Marble Falls, TX*

Sweet Potato & Bacon Fries

Sweet potatoes are so yummy all by themselves...but with a touch of bacon and a sprinkle of brown sugar, they are just the best!

Serves 6

2 to 3 large sweet potatoes, peeled and cut into
    strips or wedges
1 T. lemon juice
2 t. olive oil
½ t. salt
3 slices bacon, cut into small pieces
2 T. brown sugar, packed
¼ c. chopped pecans

Peel the sweet potatoes and cut into strips or wedges. Place potatoes in a plastic zipping bag; add lemon juice and olive oil. Shake the bag. Preheat the air fryer to 375 degrees. Working in batches, place sweet potatoes in the basket. Add bacon. Cook for about 10 to 12 minutes, shaking or turning once, until bacon is crisp and potatoes are crisp and tender. Remove from basket and sprinkle with brown sugar and chopped pecans.

Judy Skadburg, *Grand Marais, MN*

Little Piggies in a Blanket

We all love the original hot dog wrapped in dough that is called "pigs in a blanket." You will love this version using cocktail sausages and crescent-roll dough all wrapped up and cooked in your air fryer...we make them often!

Makes 2 dozen

24 cocktail sausages
8-oz. tube refrigerated crescent rolls

Lay sausages on a paper towel to remove any excess moisture. Open the tube of crescent rolls and lay out on a flat work surface. Use a knife to divide each of the rolls into 3 triangles. Wrap each triangle piece of dough around a sausage. Preheat the air fryer to 350 degrees. Working in batches, lay the wrapped sausages in the fryer in a single layer. Cook for about 5 or 6 minutes until golden, turning or shaking the basket once. Remove and continue cooking remaining sausages.

> ❧ **Make It Special** ❧
>
> Serve these wrapped piggies with a variety of sauces. Try Dijon mustard, chili sauce or chipotle sauce for a real treat.

Little Piggies in a Blanket

Instant Pot® Recipes

By now, your electric pressure cooker may be one of your favorite appliances in the kitchen, or perhaps you are new to this amazing appliance. Wherever you are in your cooking experience with this versatile cooker, you'll love the wide range of recipes that you can fix for breakfast, lunch and dinner. In this section of our cookbook, you'll find everything from Cherry Chili Chicken to Salted Caramel Cheesecake. There are classic recipes such as Easy Cheesy Shells and some recipes you may have wanted to try such as Butternut Squash Risotto or Coconut Chicken Curry. Because this multi-purpose cooker also sautés, boils eggs, and makes amazing soups, you'll find endless dishes to try for every meal of the day. So get ready to enjoy cooking in your electric pressure cooker with recipes your entire family will love.

*Based on a recipe shared by **Jill Valentine**, Jackson, TN*

Grilled Eggplant & Tomato Pasta Sauce

Both purple and white eggplants work well in this savory sauce. It's delicious served over pasta, topped with fresh basil or grated cheese.

Serves 4

1½ lbs. eggplant, sliced
½ to 1 t. salt
½ c. olive oil, divided
4 boneless, skinless chicken
    breasts, trimmed
2 onions, finely chopped
3 cloves garlic, minced
¾ lb. sliced mushrooms
6-oz. can tomato paste
28-oz. can whole plum
    tomatoes, crushed
½ c. red wine or water
1 T. dried parsley
1½ t. dried oregano
pepper to taste
cooked pasta

1 Sprinkle cut sides of eggplant with salt; drain on paper towels for 30 minutes. Brush some of the oil over eggplant and chicken breasts. Grill eggplant and chicken for about 20 minutes, until tender. Let cool. Coarsely chop eggplant. Set chicken and eggplant aside.

2 In an electric pressure cooker, choose the Sauté setting. Heat remaining oil until sizzling. Add onions and garlic and cook for about 3 minutes. Add mushrooms; cook until they release their liquid. Add tomato paste; cook and stir for one minute. Add tomatoes with juice, wine or water and seasonings; bring to a boil. Boil one minute. Press Cancel to reset pot.

3 Secure the lid and set the pressure release to Sealing. Choose Manual/High Pressure and cook on high pressure for 5 minutes. Once the cooking time is up, use Natural Release method to release pressure. Carefully open the pot. Stir in eggplant. Serve sauce over cooked pasta. Top with sliced chicken. Garnish as desired.

Grilled Eggplant & Tomato Pasta Sauce

Based on a recipe shared by **Heather Porter,** *Villa Park, IL*

Chicago Italian Beef

If you come from Chicago, you know Italian beef. Serve with chewy, delicious Italian rolls and top with some of the gravy from the pot...the taste is out of this world!

Serves 10 to 14

1 T. canola oil

3-lb. beef rump roast or bottom round roast

16-oz. jar pepperoncini or sliced peppers

16-oz. jar mild giardiniera mix in oil

14-oz. can beef broth

1-oz. pkg. Italian salad dressing mix

10 to 14 Italian round rolls, split

1 Choose the Sauté setting on the electric pressure cooker. Heat oil and brown beef on all sides. Add undrained peppers and remaining ingredients, except rolls, and stir well. Press Cancel to reset pot.

2 Secure the lid and set pressure release to Sealing. Choose the Manual/Pressure setting and cook for 40 minutes on high pressure. After cooking time is up, let the pressure release naturally. (This may take up to 30 minutes.)

3 Carefully open the pot. Remove beef with a slotted spoon. Reserve the liquid. Slice or shred the beef, removing any fat. To serve, top rolls with shredded beef and some of the liquid and vegetables.

Chicago Italian Beef

Carol Field Dahlstrom, *Ankeny, IA*

Cherry Chili Chicken

Some may think this is an unusual combination of flavors, but after you try it you will know why everyone loves it!

Serves 6

1 T. olive oil

2 lbs. boneless, skinless chicken thighs or breasts

½ c. cherry jam

½ c. water

1 T. soy sauce

1 t. fresh ginger, peeled and chopped

1 T. fresh chives, chopped

½ t. chili powder

½ t. salt

½ t. pepper

Garnish: chopped chives

1 Add oil to pot and choose the Sauté Setting. Brown the chicken on both sides for about 2 minutes. Press Cancel to reset the pot.

2 In a small bowl, whisk together jam, water, soy sauce, ginger, chives, chili powder, salt and pepper. Pour jam mixture over the chicken. Turn the chicken pieces around to coat them, arranging in a single layer.

3 Secure the lid and set the pressure release to Sealing. Choose the Pressure/Poultry setting and set the cook time for 12 minutes. After the cooking is complete, use the Natural Release method to release pressure naturally for 15 minutes and then use Venting/Quick Release to release any remaining steam.

4 Open the pot carefully and transfer cooked chicken to a platter. Spoon glaze over the chicken pieces. Garnish with chopped chives.

Cherry Chili Chicken

Based on a recipe shared by **Etha Hutchcroft,** Ames, IA

Butternut Squash Risotto

With pressure cooking you can make this impressive risotto recipe in less than 30 minutes.

Serves 4

2 T. olive oil

2 shallots, chopped

1 cloves garlic, finely chopped

2 c. Arborio rice, uncooked

4 c. chicken broth

1 lb. butternut squash, cut into
   ½-inch cubes

½ c. shredded Parmesan cheese

½ t. salt

¼ t. pepper

Garnish: chopped fresh parsley

1 Choose the Sauté setting on the electric pressure cooker. Add oil, shallots and garlic. Cook for 2 minutes, stirring occasionally. Add rice and cook 2 minutes, stirring. Press Cancel to reset pot.

2 Add broth and squash. Secure lid and set pressure release to Sealing. Select Manual/Pressure Cook and cook at high pressure for 7 minutes. Once cooking is complete, carefully move the release to Venting/Quick Release to manually release any remaining pressure. Carefully open the pot.

3 Stir in cheese, salt, and pepper. Let stand 5 minutes before serving. Garnish with parsley.

Butternut Squash Risotto

Base on a recipe shared by **Joni Bitting,** *Papillion, NE*

Grandpa's Pork Tacos

We love to make these tacos on the weekend and have friends over to watch the game, play cards or visit. We just set out the makin's and let everyone make their own.

Makes 10 servings, 2 tacos each

2 T. olive oil

4-lb. pork shoulder roast

¾ c. onion, chopped

1 T. garlic, minced

10-oz. can diced tomatoes with green chiles

½ c. chicken broth

1 T. chili powder

1 T. ground cumin

1 t. Spanish paprika

salt and pepper to taste

20 crisp corn taco shells

Garnish: sour cream, sliced avocado, diced tomatoes, fresh cilantro, shredded cheese, shredded lettuce

1 Add oil to a skillet over medium heat; brown roast on both sides, 3 to 4 minutes. Remove roast and place in electric pressure cooker; set aside.

2 Sauté onion and garlic in skillet for 3 minutes; add to pot. Add tomatoes with juice, broth and spices to pot. Secure the lid and set the pressure release to Sealing. Select Manual/Pressure and cook for 45 minutes on high pressure. Once the cooking time is up, use the Natural Release method for 10 minutes, then use Venting/Quick Release method to release any remaining pressure. Carefully open the pot. Remove pork from pot and shred. Season as desired with salt and pepper. Serve pork in taco shells, garnished as desired.

Grandpa's Pork Tacos

Based on a recipe shared by **Elizabeth Burnley,** *Ankeny, IA*

Rainbow Chard with Cranberries & Nuts

The color of the rainbow chard and the cranberries makes this vegetarian dish pretty and unique. The crunch of the walnuts and carrots adds the perfect texture.

Serves 4 to 6

1 T. olive oil
½ red onion, sliced
1 clove garlic, chopped
½ t. red pepper flakes
½ c. carrot, peeled and
   shredded
8 c. rainbow chard, stems
   sliced, and leaves cut into
   ½-inch-wide strips
½ c. dried cranberries
½ c. chicken broth
¼ c. chopped walnuts, toasted

1 Select Sauté setting and add oil. Add onion, garlic and red pepper flakes and cook for about one minute. Add the carrot and sliced Swiss chard stems; sauté for about 5 minutes, or until softened. Stir in chard, cranberries and broth. Press Cancel to reset pot.

2 Secure the lid and set the pressure release to Sealing. Select Manual/Pressure setting and cook for 3 minutes on high pressure. After cooking time is up, release pressure carefully using the Venting/Quick Release method. Carefully open the pot.

3 Transfer to a serving dish. Top with walnuts and serve immediately.

Rainbow Chard with Cranberries & Nuts

Based on a recipe shared by **Claire Bertram,** Lexington, KY

Down-Home Soup Beans

There is nothing better than soup beans on a chilly day!

Serves 8

1 T. oil
1 onion, diced
1 c. carrot, peeled and sliced
1 clove garlic, minced
¼ t. red pepper flakes
1 to 1½ c. cooked ham, diced
1 lb. dried Great Northern
   or pinto beans, rinsed and
   sorted
8 c. vegetable or low-sodium
   chicken broth
½ t. salt
1 t. pepper
Garnish: chopped fresh parsley

1 Select Sauté setting on the electric pressure cooker and add the oil, onion, carrot, garlic and red pepper flakes. Sauté until softened, about 5 minutes. Add ham and sauté about 5 minutes. Add beans, broth, salt and pepper. Press Cancel to reset pot.

2 Secure the lid and set the pressure release to Sealing. Press the Bean/Chili setting or use Manual/Pressure setting. Cook for 50 minutes at high pressure.

3 After the cooking time is up, let the pressure release naturally (this will take about 30 minutes). Open the pot and ladle into small bowls. Garnish with parsley.

Down-Home Soup Beans

Based on a recipe shared by **Allison May,** *Seattle, WA*

Vietnamese Pho-Style Chicken Soup

There are many variations of this Asian soup, and we like this one best. It is not too spicy, and has just the right amount of fresh ingredients and spices. Enjoy!

Serves 4

8 c. chicken broth

4 boneless, skinless chicken thighs

2 T. fresh ginger, peeled and chopped

5 star anise pods

3 whole cloves

2 c. water

$^2/_3$ c. sticky or sushi rice, uncooked and rinsed

2 T. fish sauce

2 t. brown sugar, packed

Garnish: sliced green onions, jalapeños, fresh cilantro

1 In the electric pressure cooker, combine broth, chicken, ginger, anise pods, cloves and water. Secure the lid. Set pressure release to Sealing. Select Manual/Pressure and cook on high pressure for 9 minutes. After cooking time is up, allow pressure to release naturally for 10 minutes; then release the remaining pressure manually using the Venting/Quick Release method. Open the pot. Remove chicken and transfer to a plate.

2 Remove solids from the broth with a slotted spoon or sieve. Stir the rice, fish sauce and sugar into the broth. Secure lid and set the pressure release to Sealing. Select Manual/Pressure and cook on high pressure for one minute. After cooking time is up, allow the pressure to release naturally using the Natural Release method. Carefully open the pot.

3 Shred the chicken and return it to the pot; stir. Ladle soup into individual bowls; top with green onions, jalapeños and cilantro.

Vietnamese Pho-Style
Chicken Soup

Based on a recipe shared by **Sharon Tillman,** *Hampton, VA*

Smoked Sausage & White Bean Soup

I love to make this hearty soup on autumn weekends, after my friend Samantha and I come back from antiquing and seeing the fall colors. With a basket of warm, crusty bread, it's a meal in itself.

Serves 6

1 lb. dried navy beans, rinsed and sorted

1 to 2 T. olive oil

1 lb. smoked turkey sausage, sliced

½ onion, diced

2 cloves garlic, minced

3 carrots, peeled and chopped

2 stalks celery, chopped

1 t. fresh thyme, chopped

2 t. fresh rosemary, chopped

7 c. vegetable broth

3 c. fresh baby spinach

1 t. salt

¼ t. pepper

1 Place beans in a deep bowl; add enough water to cover by 2 inches. Soak for 8 hours or overnight. Drain; rinse and set aside.

2 Select Sauté setting on electric pressure cooker. Add oil and cook sausage until browned; drain. Add onion; sauté until translucent. Add garlic; sauté for one minute. Press Cancel to reset pot.

3 Add beans and remaining ingredients; stir. Secure lid and set to Sealing. Select Soup/Broth setting and set time for 20 minutes. After cooking time is up, let pressure release naturally for 5 minutes, then use Venting/Quick Release method to release remaining pressure. Carefully open the pot.

4 To thicken the soup, use a wooden spoon to mash some of the beans against the side of the pot.

**Smoked Sausage &
White Bean Soup**

*Based on a recipe shared by **Alison Carbonara,** Grove City, OH*

Steak & Red Pepper Bowls

This is such a pretty dish to serve and so satisfying. We like to use yellow rice, but you can use white or brown rice as well.

Serves 6

2½ lbs. beef chuck roast, thinly
   sliced and fat trimmed
1 t. salt, divided
1 t. pepper, divided
3 T. olive oil, divided
3 red peppers, sliced
1 yellow onion, sliced
2 c. beef broth
3 T. soy sauce
2 T. tomato paste
5-oz. pkg. yellow rice, cooked
Garnish: fresh cilantro, sour
   cream

1 Sprinkle beef with ½ teaspoon each salt and pepper. Choose the Sauté setting and heat one tablespoon oil until hot. Brown half of the beef on both sides, about one minute per side, for about 3 to 4 minutes. Remove beef to a plate with juices. Repeat with remaining beef and one tablespoon olive oil; remove to plate.

2 Add remaining oil and sauté peppers and onion until fragrant, about 3 to 4 minutes. Return meat and juices to pot, stirring to combine. Press Cancel to reset pot.

3 In a bowl, whisk together broth, soy sauce and tomato paste; pour broth mixture over all. Secure the lid and set pressure release to Sealing. Choose the Manual/Pressure function and cook for 10 minutes at high pressure. After the cooking time is up, use the Natural Release method for 10 minutes and then release remaining pressure manually using Venting/Quick Release method. Open pot carefully.

4 To serve, divide rice among 4 bowls. Using a slotted spoon, top with beef and vegetables. Garnish with cilantro and sour cream.

Steak & Red Pepper Bowls

*Based on a recipe shared by **Jason Keller,** Carrollton, GA*

Spareribs with Smoky Tomato BBQ Sauce

No need to precook the ribs in boiling water...your pressure cooker does the job for you! Just add coleslaw and a pot of baked beans for a fantastic picnic meal.

Serves 4 to 6

3-lb. rack pork spareribs, skin removed, cut into 2-rib serving-size portions
salt and pepper to taste
1 to 2 T. olive oil
1 onion, thickly sliced
1 c. water

1 Prepare Smoky Tomato BBQ Sauce ahead of time; chill.

2 Season ribs with salt and pepper; set aside. Choose the Sauté setting on the electric pressure cooker and heat oil until very hot. Working in batches, add ribs in a single layer; cook until browned on both sides, 5 to 7 minutes per batch, adding oil as needed. Transfer browned ribs to a plate. Add onion to drippings in pot and cook until soft, about 3 minutes. Return ribs to pot; add any juices from plate. Add water and sauce; toss to coat ribs. Press Cancel to reset pot.

3 Secure lid and set the pressure release to Sealing. Choose Manual/Pressure and cook for 25 minutes at high pressure. Once cooking time is done, use Natural Release method to release pressure. Carefully open pot. Let stand for 15 minutes. Ribs should be falling-apart tender. Transfer ribs to a serving platter; skim fat from sauce and spoon over ribs.

SMOKY TOMATO BBQ SAUCE:

1 c. catsup
¼ c. apricot preserves
¼ c. cider vinegar
3 T. tomato paste
2 T. red wine or water
2 T. olive oil
2 T. soy sauce
1 T. dry mustard
1 T. onion powder
2 t. smoked paprika
1 clove garlic, pressed

1 Combine all ingredients in a small bowl; whisk until smooth. Cover and refrigerate.

Spareribs with Smoky Tomato BBQ Sauce

Based on a recipe shared by **June Sabatinos,** *Salt Lake City, UT*

Brown Sugar Baked Beans

Using a pressure cooker is a quick way to make a delicious scratch version of this holiday potluck classic. There are never any leftovers!

Serves 6 to 8

1 lb. dried navy beans, rinsed
　and sorted
10 c. water, divided
1 T. plus 2 t. salt, divided
8 slices thick-cut bacon, cut
　into ½-inch pieces
1 yellow onion, diced
½ c. molasses
1 c. tomato purée, crushed
½ c. brown sugar, packed
2 t. dry mustard
1 t. pepper
Optional: salt and pepper to
　taste

1 In a large bowl, combine beans, 8 cups water and one tablespoon salt. Soak for 8 hours or overnight. Drain and rinse beans; set aside.

2 Choose the Sauté setting and add bacon. Cook until crisp, about 5 minutes. Using a slotted spoon, remove bacon and transfer to a paper towel-lined plate. Add onion to bacon drippings; cook until tender, about 3 minutes. Add remaining water and salt, molasses, tomato purée, brown sugar, dry mustard and pepper; stir to combine. Stir in beans. Press Cancel to reset pot.

3 Secure lid and set to pressure release to Sealing. Select Beans or Manual/High pressure and cook for 20 minutes at high pressure. After cooking time is up, use the Natural Release method to release pressure. Carefully open lid. Press Cancel to reset pot.

4 Select Sauté setting and simmer, uncovered, for about 10 minutes, until sauce is reduced and thickened. Season with more salt and pepper, if desired.

Brown Sugar Baked Beans

Carol Field Dahlstrom, *Ankeny, IA*

Beets with Dill Sauce

This dish will impress your family & friends in so many ways...it is beautiful, delicious and full of healthy nutrients. Enjoy every bite!

Serves 4

6 to 8 medium beets in desired colors
1. c. water
1 lemon
1 T. olive oil
1 c. plain yogurt
1 T. sour cream
1 t. salt
3 T. fresh dill, chopped
coarse pepper to taste

1 Remove greens from beets and scrub beets under warm water. Pour water into the electric pressure cooker. Add the steamer basket and put the beets in the basket.

2 Secure the lid and set pressure release on Sealing. Choose Manual/Pressure and cook on high pressure for 30 minutes. After cooking time is up, let the pressure release naturally using the Natural Release method.

3 Transfer the beets to a bowl and let cool slightly. While still warm, remove the skin. Cut the beets into wedges and arrange on a platter or in bowl. Grate the zest off the lemon and set aside. Cut the lemon into wedges; squeeze juice over beets. Drizzle beets with olive oil.

4 In a small bowl, whisk together yogurt, sour cream, salt and reserved lemon zest. Drizzle the dressing over beets and top with dill and ground pepper.

Beets with Dill Sauce

Judy Bailey, *Des Moines, IA*

Hard-Cooked Eggs

We love hard-cooked eggs any time of day and you can make them easily in your electric pressure cooker. You can use the metal wire trivet that comes with your pressure cooker or there are special egg inserts or steamer baskets you can buy, but the trivet works just fine. The most remarkable thing about cooking eggs this way is that they peel so easily!

Serves 4 to 6

1 c. water
8 to 10 eggs
Garnish: coarse salt, cracked
   pepper, chopped chives

1 Place the water in the pot. Put the metal trivet or steamer basket in the pot on top of the water and carefully place the eggs in it.
Note: Don't place the eggs in the water, put them on top of the water.

2 Secure the lid and set the pressure release to Sealing. Choose Manual/Pressure for 6 minutes at high pressure. After cooking time is up, use the Natural Release method for 2 minutes then Venting/Quick Release method until the pressure is released. Adjust the time based on your desired doneness.

3 Carefully remove the eggs with a spoon or scoop and place in ice water. Peel the eggs right away or refrigerate and peel when ready to eat. Garnish as desired.

Hard-Cooked Eggs

*Based on a recipe shared by **Amy Butcher,** Columbus, GA*

Asian Lettuce Wraps

Cooking pork in your electric pressure cooker is so easy and it shreds nicely for wraps or sandwiches of any kind. You can vary the spices you use to fit your liking.

Serves 8

2 t. sesame oil
2 green onions, chopped
1 clove garlic, minced
1 T. fresh ginger, peeled and
  minced
8-oz. pkg. mushrooms, chopped
2 lbs. pork loin, cut into 2-inch
  chunks
1 c. chicken broth
⅓ c. soy sauce
⅓ c. balsamic vinegar
½ t. red pepper flakes
1 T. honey
2 T. cornstarch
3 T. water
large lettuce leaves such as bib
  or leaf lettuce
Garnish: green onions, sesame
  seeds, shredded carrot

1 Choose the Sauté function and add oil, onions, garlic, ginger and mushrooms. Sauté about 2 minutes until mushrooms start to brown. Add the pork, broth, soy sauce, vinegar, pepper flakes and honey to the pot. Stir gently to mix; brown, about 2 minutes. Press Cancel to reset pot.

2 Set the pressure release to Sealing. Select Manual/Pressure and cook for 35 minutes on high pressure. Once the timer is up, let the pot naturally release pressure for 10 minutes, then use Venting/Quick Release to release any remaining pressure.

3 Remove pork and shred it; set aside. In a small bowl, mix together cornstarch and water. Choose the Sauté function and once the liquid in the pot is boiling, add the cornstarch mixture. Boil for one to 2 minutes, until the sauce has thickened. Add the pork back to the pot and stir well to coat. Press Cancel to reset pot.

4 Serve pork on lettuce leaves. Garnish with green onions, sesame seeds and carrots.

Asian Lettuce Wraps

Based on a recipe shared by **Kelley Nicholson,** *Gooseberry Patch*

Risotto with Italian Sausage & Kale

Zesty Italian flavors make this a popular choice for casual weeknight dinners. A tossed green salad and some crusty bread round out the meal nicely.

Makes 2 to 3 servings

1 T. olive oil
½ lb. sweet or hot Italian ground pork sausage
1 T. butter
½ c. onion, chopped
3 c. fresh kale, stemmed and chopped
½ t. salt
¼ t. red pepper flakes
1 c. Arborio rice, uncooked
⅓ c. white wine or broth
2¼ c. chicken or vegetable broth
⅔ c. shredded Parmesan cheese, divided

1 Choose the Sauté setting on the electric pressure cooker and heat oil over medium-high heat until very hot. Add sausage and cook until browned. Drain, reserving one tablespoon drippings in pot; add butter and onion. Cook until onion is softened, about 3 minutes. Stir in kale and seasonings. Add rice; stir to coat. Pour in wine or broth; scrape up browned bits from bottom of pot. Stir in chicken or vegetable broth. Press Cancel to reset pot.

2 Secure the lid and set the pressure release to Sealing. Choose the Manual/Pressure setting and cook for 7 minutes on high pressure. After cooking time is up, use Natural Release method to release pressure for 3 minutes, then use the Venting/Quick Release method to release any remaining pressure. Carefully open the pot.

3 Stir in ⅓ cup cheese; season with more salt, if desired. Serve at once, topped with remaining cheese.

Risotto with Italian Sausage & Kale

*Based on a recipe shared by **Jennie Hempfling,** Columbus, OH*

Coconut Chicken Curry

This goes very well with fragrant basmati rice. I usually cook the rice first, put it in a bowl and cover it while I cook the chicken. If you don't have all the spices, substitute some curry powder along with the salt and pepper.

Serves 4

2 T. olive oil

1 onion, diced

5 t. garlic, minced

1 t. fresh ginger, peeled and minced

1½ lbs. boneless, skinless chicken thighs, cut into quarters, or chicken breasts, cut into 2-inch cubes

1 t. paprika

1 t. turmeric

1 t. ground coriander

1 t. garam masala

¼ t. cayenne pepper

¼ t. ground cumin

1 t. salt

¼ t. pepper

15-oz. can tomato sauce

2 green peppers, coarsely chopped

½ c. canned coconut milk

cooked rice

Garnish: chopped fresh parsley or cilantro, freshly shaved coconut

1 Press the Sauté setting on electric pressure cooker; add oil and onion. Cook for 5 to 6 minute, until tender and translucent. Stir in garlic, ginger, chicken, spices, salt and pepper; cook for one to 2 minutes, until fragrant. Stir in tomato sauce. Press Cancel to reset pot.

2 Close and lock the lid and set the pressure release to Sealing. Select the Manual/Pressure setting and cook for 8 minutes on high pressure. After cooking time is up, use the Venting/Quick Release method to release pressure. Carefully open the pot.

3 Choose the Sauté setting and add green peppers; simmer to desired tenderness, about 3 minutes. Stir in coconut milk. Press Cancel to reset pot.

4 Serve over cooked rice; garnish as desired.

Coconut Chicken Curry

Based on a recipe shared by **Henry Burnley,** *Ankeny, IA*

Easy Cheesy Shells

Everyone loves mac & cheese! Choose the shape of pasta your family likes and add tasty toppings to make it extra special.

Serves 4

2 T. butter
8-oz. pkg. pasta shells,
   uncooked
1 c. whole milk
1 c. water
½ c. whipping cream
¾ c. cream cheese, softened
½ t. dry mustard
¼ t. cayenne pepper
½ t. salt
½ t. pepper
8-oz. pkg. shredded sharp
   Cheddar cheese
Garnish: coarse pepper,
   chopped green onion,
   paprika

1 Select the Sauté setting and melt butter in the electric pressure cooker. Add pasta shells and sauté for 2 to 3 minutes. Press Cancel to reset the pot.

2 In a bowl, combine the milk, water, cream, cream cheese and seasonings; mix thoroughly. Add cream cheese mixture to the pasta in the pot.

3 Secure the lid and set the pressure release to Sealing. Select the Manual/High Pressure setting and cook for 6 minutes. Carefully release the pressure using Venting/ Quick Release. Stir in Cheddar cheese, adding more milk if mixture appears dry. Garnish with pepper, green onion or paprika.

Easy Cheesy Shells

*Based on a recipe shared by **Lyne Neymeyer,** Des Moines, IA*

Easy Mongolian Beef

Using an electric pressure cooker for this dish works so well because you can sauté the beef and spices to get the carmelized flavor and then cook it quickly to make it tender.

Serves 4 to 6

2 T. olive oil, divided

2 lbs. beef sirloin steak, sliced ½-inch thick, divided

½ t. salt, divided

½ t. pepper, divided

3 cloves garlic, minced

1 t. fresh ginger, peeled and minced

2 small onions, sliced

3 T. soy sauce

3 T. brown sugar

1 ¼ c. water

2 T. all-purpose flour

½ c. beef broth

cooked rice

Garnish: sliced green onions, red pepper flakes

1 Select the Sauté setting on the electric pressure cooker and heat one tablespoon oil. Add half of the beef slices; season with half each of the salt and pepper. Sear the beef for 5 to 6 minutes on each side, until browned. Repeat with remaining beef, salt and pepper.

2 Add garlic, ginger, and onions. Sauté for 2 to 3 minutes. Add soy sauce, brown sugar and water to the pot and stir all ingredients together. Press the Cancel function to reset pot.

3 Secure the lid and set the pressure release to Sealing. Choose Manual/Pressure and set on high pressure for 15 minutes. Once the cooking is complete, use the Natural Release method for 10 minutes, then release any remaining pressure manually using Venting/Quick Release method. Carefully open the lid.

4 Mix together flour and broth and add to the pot. Choose the Sauté function and simmer until the sauce thickens. Transfer to serving bowl and serve over cooked rice. Garnish with green onions and red pepper flakes.

Easy Mongolian Beef

Based on a recipe shared by **Lynn Williams,** *Muncie, IN*

Pulled Pork Sandwiches

We usually make this pulled pork for sandwiches, but sometimes we enjoy it for tacos, burritos, or on warm lettuce salads. It is good any way you use it!

Serves 8

3 T. olive oil

2 lbs. pork shoulder, fat trimmed

½ c. onion, chopped

1 c. chicken broth

½ c. tomato paste

1 T. lemon juice

1 t. salt

1 t. pepper

1 t. smoked paprika

toasted buns, split

Optional: favorite coleslaw

1 Select the Sauté setting and add the oil. Add the pork and sear on both sides, for about 8 minutes total. Add the onion and sauté for another 2 minutes. Press the Cancel function to reset the pot. Add the broth, tomato paste, lemon juice, salt, pepper and paprika; stir well.

2 Secure the lid and set pressure release to Sealing. Select Manual/Pressure and cook on high pressure for 45 minutes. Once cooking is complete, let the pressure release naturally for 10 minutes. Release any remaining pressure manually using the Venting/Quick Release method.

3 Open the pot; transfer the pork to a plate. Shred the pork and return to the pot. Select Sauté setting and cook for 5 minutes more to reduce liquid. Press Cancel to reset the pot. Remove pork from pot and serve on toasted buns, topped with coleslaw if desired.

Pulled Pork Sandwiches

*Based on a recipe shared by **Gloria Heigh,** Santa Fe, NM*

Quinoa Bowls with Swiss Chard & Poached Egg

We love to serve this quick-to-fix recipe on weekends when we have a little more time to enjoy every bite! Clean-up is easy and we have a hearty meal to start the day.

Serves 4

1 c. quinoa, uncooked, rinsed
   and drained
2 c. plus 2 T. water
1 t. salt
5 to 6 T. olive oil, divided
½ onion, chopped
1 carrot, peeled and sliced
6 c. Swiss chard, stems chopped
   and leaves coarsely chopped
1 clove garlic, minced
1 c. sliced mushrooms
2 T. water
1 t. salt
2 t. vinegar
4 eggs
pepper to taste
2 T. fresh chives, chopped

1 Combine quinoa, 2 cups water and salt in the electric pressure cooker. Secure the lid and set the pressure release to Sealing. Select the Multigrain setting and set the cooking time for 8 minutes on high pressure. After the cooking time is up, let the pressure release naturally for 10 minutes and then carefully release any remaining pressure using Venting/Quick Release method. Open the pot and stir the quinoa. Remove quinoa from the pot and cover to keep warm. Rinse the pot and return to cooker.

2 Choose the Sauté setting. Heat one tablespoon oil in the pot and add onion, carrot and Swiss chard stems; cook, stirring often, until softened, about 5 minutes. Add garlic and mushrooms; cook until mushrooms are softened, about 2 to 3 minutes, adding more oil if needed. Place chard leaves on top of onion mixture; add remaining 2 tablespoons water and salt. Cook until leaves wilt, about 3 minutes; stir in quinoa. Press Cancel to reset the pot. Divide mixture between 4 bowls; set aside.

3 To a saucepan over medium heat, add vinegar and 2 inches water; bring to a simmer. Crack one egg into a saucer. Using a slotted spoon, swirl simmering water in a circle; slowly add egg. Cook until yolk is softly set. Remove with a slotted spoon and place on top of one quinoa bowl. Repeat with other eggs. Drizzle each bowl with one tablespoon remaining oil; sprinkle with pepper and chives.

Quinoa Bowls with Swiss Chard &
Poached Egg

Based on a recipe shared by **Kimberlee Eakins,** *Cleveland, OH*

Salted Caramel Cheesecake

You'll love this creamy cheesecake! The flaked salt is optional, but I really like the salty-sweet taste.

Serves 6

2 8-oz. pkgs. cream cheese,
    room temperature
½ c. light brown sugar, packed
¼ c. sour cream
1 T. all-purpose flour
½ t. salt
1½ t. vanilla extract
2 eggs, beaten
2 c. water
Garnish: ½ c. caramel topping
Optional: 1 t. flaked sea salt

1 Make Buttery Cracker Crust; set aside. In a bowl, beat cream cheese and brown sugar with an electric mixer on medium speed until blended. Add sour cream; beat for 30 more seconds. Beat in flour, salt and vanilla. Add eggs; beat until just smooth. Pour mixture into crust. Place a length of aluminum foil underneath pan. Wrap foil over bottom of pan. Fold a long piece of foil in half lengthwise; center pan on foil strip.

2 Pour water into an electric pressure cooker; add a rack or trivet. Using the foil as handles, place pan into pot. Secure and set the pressure release to Sealing. Choose the Manual/Pressure setting and cook for 25 minutes at high pressure. After the cooking time is up, use the Natural Release method to release pressure. Open lid.

3 Using oven mitts, remove pan from pot using foil handles; set on a wire rack and cool for one hour. Cover cheesecake in pan with foil. Refrigerate at least 4 hours or overnight.

4 At serving time, loosen sides of cheesecake from pan with a table knife, release sides of the pan. Cut into wedges. Garnish with caramel topping, and sea salt, if desired.

BUTTERY CRACKER CRUST:

1½ c. buttery round crackers,
    finely crushed
¼ c. butter, melted
2 T. sugar

1 Spray a 7" springform pan lightly with non-stick vegetable spray. Line with a 7-inch circle of parchment paper; spray again and set aside. Combine all ingredients; mix well. Press mixture firmly into bottom and up sides of pan.

Salted Caramel Cheesecake

Judy Skadburg, Grand Marais, MN

Poached Pears & Cranberries

This makes a beautiful and light dessert and is so quick to make. Try it with apples if you like...just steam for 2 more minutes.

Serves 4

4 c. water
⅓ c. honey
⅓ c. brown sugar, packed
¼ t. cinnamon
1 lemon
4 firm pears, peeled, cored and
   cut in half
⅓ c. dried cranberries
Optional: yogurt, ice cream,
   cottage cheese

1 Select Sauté setting on the electric pressure cooker and add the water, honey, brown sugar and cinnamon. Use a zester to add the lemon zest to the pot, then halve the lemon and squeeze the juice into the pot. Bring to a simmer. While the liquid is simmering, add the pears. Press Cancel to reset the pot.

2 Secure the lid and set the pressure release to Sealing. Select the Steam setting and set at high pressure for one minute. Carefully use the Venting/Quick Release method to release pressure. Open the pot and remove the pears; place in a bowl.

3 Choose the Sauté setting and add the cranberries. Allow the liquid to cook, reducing to about half. This should take about 10 minutes. Press Cancel to reset the pot. Ladle the reduced liquid over the pears. Cover and refrigerate for at least 4 hours before serving. Serve over plain yogurt, ice cream or cottage cheese, if desired.

Poached Pears & Cranberries

Carol Field Dahlstrom, *Ankeny, IA*

Chocolate Mocha Cake

This little cake is perfect for a small get-together and is simply delicious!

Serves 6

2⅓ c. water
1 c. all-purpose flour
⅔ c. brown sugar, packed
⅓ c. baking cocoa
1 t. baking powder
½ t. baking soda
1 T. instant coffee granules
½ t. salt
3 eggs
⅓ c. plain Greek yogurt
4 T. butter, melted and cooled
¾ c. dark chocolate chips
Garnish: powdered sugar,
    baking cocoa

1 Grease a 7" Bundt® pan with non-stick vegetable spray. Fold a strip of aluminum foil in half and in half again lengthwise to form a piece about 20 inches long and 3 inches wide, to serve as a sling for the pan for lifting it out. Pour water into pot and put the trivet in the pot.

2 In a bowl, mix together flour, sugar, cocoa, baking powder, baking soda, coffee and salt. Add the eggs, yogurt and butter; whisk until well mixed. Stir in the chocolate chips and mix. Batter will be thick. Spoon the batter evenly into the prepared pan.

3 Holding the ends of the foil sling holder, lift the Bundt® pan and lower into the pot. Fold over the ends of the foil so they fit inside the pot. Secure lid and set pressure release to Sealing. Select the Manual/Pressure or Cake setting and set the cooking time for 40 minutes at high pressure.

4 After the cooking time is up, use the Natural Release method for 10 minutes, then carefully use the Venting/ Quick Release method to release any remaining pressure. Open the pot and wearing oven mitts, grasp the ends of the foil sling to lift the cake from the pot. Set cake on a cooling rack, then invert cake on the rack. Dust with powdered sugar or baking cocoa.

Chocolate Mocha Cake

Slow-Cooker Recipes

Your trusty slow cooker has been a staple in your kitchen for years. You love the ease it brings to preparing meals ahead and having them cook while you go about your day. It quietly cooks for you and the results are always so rewarding. In this chapter featuring this all-time-favorite appliance, we bring you some new recipes to add to your family favorites. You'll love Pepperoni-Pizza Rigatoni and Slow-Cooker Country Chicken & Dumplings. Soups are always a great slow-cooker choice, and you'll love our Slow-Cooker Butternut Squash Soup and delicious New England Clam Chowder. And if you want a sweet treat, your slow cooker can help out there too. Crockery Apple Pie and The Easiest Rice Pudding finish a meal with the perfect touch of sweetness. So grab that favorite slow cooker and try some tasty new flavors...they'll make you love this old stand-by appliance even more.

Lynda Robson, *Boston, MA*

Overnight Cherry Oatmeal

Assemble the night before and wake to the aroma of cherry pie...what a great way to start the day!

Serves 4 to 6

3 c. long-cooking oats, uncooked
¾ c. powdered sugar
¼ t. salt
21-oz. can cherry pie filling
6 c. water
1 t. almond extract

Combine oats, powdered sugar and salt in a large bowl; pour into a slow cooker that has been sprayed with non-stick vegetable spray. Add remaining ingredients; stir until combined. Cover and cook on low setting for 6 to 8 hours.

~ **Making it Special** ~

Early risers will appreciate a crockery cooker of Overnight Cherry Oatmeal! Set out brown sugar and a small bottle of cream on ice so everyone can top their own.

Pamela Lome, *Buffalo Grove, IL*

Easy Beef Goulash

This is a rich and hearty dish they will love.

Serves 6

½ c. all-purpose flour
1 T. paprika
salt and pepper to taste
1½ lbs. beef chuck roast, cut into 1-inch cubes
1 T. olive oil
6-oz. can tomato paste
½ t. dried oregano
½ t. dried basil
1 small red onion, sliced
¾ c. beef broth

Combine flour, paprika, salt and pepper in a small bowl. Dredge beef cubes in mixture; brown beef in hot oil in a skillet. Place beef in a slow cooker; top with tomato paste, herbs and onion. Add just enough beef broth to cover meat; stir to blend. Cover and cook on low setting for 5 to 6 hours.

Easy Beef Goulash

Jessica Robertson, *Fishers, IN*

Slow-Cooker Hashbrown Casserole

This will become your go-to dinner on those busy game nights!

Serves 8

32-oz. pkg. frozen shredded hashbrowns
1 lb. ground pork sausage, browned and drained
1 onion, diced
1 green pepper, diced
1½ c. shredded Cheddar cheese
1 doz. eggs, beaten
1 c. milk
¼ t. salt
1 t. pepper

Place ⅓ each of hashbrowns, sausage, onion, green pepper and cheese in a lightly greased slow cooker. Repeat layering 2 more times, ending with cheese. Beat eggs, milk, salt and pepper together in a large bowl; pour over top. Cover and cook on low setting for 6 hours.

Julie Pak, *Henryetta, OK*

Smoky Sausage Dinner

Away from home all day? This slow-cooker creation will have dinner waiting for you!

Serves 6

5 potatoes, peeled and quartered
1 head cabbage, coarsely chopped into bite-size pieces
16-oz. pkg. baby carrots
1 onion, thickly sliced into wedges
salt and pepper to taste
14-oz. pkg. smoked pork sausage, sliced into 2-inch pieces
½ c. water
Garnish: fresh parsley

Spray a 5 to 6-quart slow cooker with non-stick vegetable spray. Layer vegetables, sprinkling each layer with salt and pepper. Place sausage on top. Pour water down one side of slow cooker. Cover and cook on low setting for 6 to 8 hours. Garnish with fresh parsley.

> ⟿ **Savvy Side** ⟿
>
> A fruit salad is the perfect side with this hashbrown casserole. Combine one cup each sliced strawberries, blueberries, raspberries and chopped celery with ½ c. chopped pecans. Toss with balsamic vinegar dressing. Yum!

Smoky Sausage Dinner

Tina Goodpasture, *Meadowview, VA*

Slow-Cooked Pulled Pork

A southern-style sandwich favorite! Enjoy it like we do, served with coleslaw and dill pickles.

Makes 12 sandwiches

1 T. oil
3½ to 4-lb. boneless pork shoulder roast, tied
10 ½-oz. can French onion soup
1 c. catsup
¼ c. cider vinegar
Optional: 2 T. brown sugar, packed
bread slices or rolls

Heat oil in a skillet over medium heat. Add roast and brown on all sides; remove to a large slow cooker and set aside. Mix soup, catsup and vinegar. Add brown sugar if using; pour over roast. Cover and cook on low setting for 8 to 10 hours, until roast is fork-tender. Remove roast to a platter; discard string and let stand for 10 minutes. Shred roast, using 2 forks; return to slow cooker and stir. Spoon meat and sauce onto bread slices or rolls.

Joanne Curran, *Arlington, MA*

Slow-Cooker Country Chicken & Dumplings

Everyone loves chicken and dumplings! Using refrigerated biscuits for the dumplings and a slow cooker to cook makes this recipe a lifesaver on busy weeknights.

Serves 6 to 8

4 boneless, skinless chicken breasts, cut up and
   browned
2 10 ¾-oz. cans cream of chicken soup
2 T. butter, sliced
1 onion, finely diced
1 c. frozen peas
2 7 ½-oz. tubes refrigerated biscuits, torn
Garnish: chopped parsley

Place chicken, soup, butter and onion in a 4-quart slow cooker; add enough water to cover chicken. Cover and cook on high setting for 4 hours. Add peas and biscuits to slow cooker; gently push biscuits into cooking liquid. Cover and continue cooking for about 1½ hours, until biscuits are done in the center. Garnish with chopped parsley.

Stephanie Norton, *Saginaw, TX*

Nana's Slow-Cooker Meatballs

These meatballs have been famous in my family for generations and are begged for at parties by young and old alike. Use a slow cooker for easy prep and to keep them warm.

Makes 4 dozen

2½ c. catsup
1 c. brown sugar, packed
2 T. Worcestershire sauce
2 lbs. ground beef
1.35-oz. pkg. onion soup mix
5-oz. can evaporated milk

Combine catsup, brown sugar and Worcestershire sauce in a slow cooker; stir well and cover. Turn slow cooker to high setting and allow mixture to warm while preparing the meatballs. Combine beef, onion soup mix and evaporated milk; mix well and form into one-inch balls. Place meatballs on an ungreased 15"x10" jelly-roll pan. Bake at 325 degrees for 20 minutes; drain. Spoon meatballs into slow cooker and reduce setting to low. Cover and cook 2 to 3 hours, stirring gently after one hour.

Dana Cunningham, *Lafayette, LA*

Slow-Cooker Butternut Squash Soup

Just chop a few ingredients and combine in the slow cooker for a delicious gourmet soup....so easy!

Serves 8

2½ lbs. butternut squash, peeled, halved, seeded and cubed
2 c. leeks, chopped
2 Granny Smith apples, peeled, cored and diced
2 14½-oz. cans chicken broth
1 c. water
seasoned salt and white pepper to taste
Garnish: freshly ground nutmeg and sour cream

Combine squash, leeks, apples, broth and water in a 4-quart slow cooker. Cover and cook on high setting for 4 hours or until squash and leeks are tender. Carefully purée the hot soup in 3 or 4 batches in a food processor or blender until smooth. Add seasoned salt and white pepper. Garnish with nutmeg and sour cream.

Slow-Cooker Butternut Squash Soup

Cindy Bunch, *Pottsboro, TX*

Poppy Seed Chicken

Don't be tempted to sprinkle on the cracker-crumb mixture while the chicken is in the slow cooker...condensation will make the topping soggy.

Serves 6

6 boneless, skinless chicken breasts
2 10¾-oz. cans cream of chicken soup
1 c. milk
1 T. poppy seed
36 round buttery crackers, crushed
¼ c. butter, melted

Place chicken in a lightly greased slow cooker. Whisk together soup, milk and poppy seed in a medium bowl; pour over chicken. Cover and cook on high setting for one hour. Reduce heat to low setting and cook, covered, 3 hours. Combine cracker crumbs and butter in a bowl, stirring until crumbs are moistened. Sprinkle over chicken just before serving.

Jo Ann, *Gooseberry Patch*

Pepperoni-Pizza Rigatoni

Personalize this recipe by adding mushrooms, black olives or any of your family's other favorite pizza toppings.

Makes 6 servings

1½ lbs. ground beef, browned and drained
8-oz. pkg. rigatoni, cooked
16-oz. pkg. shredded mozzarella cheese
10¾-oz. can cream of tomato soup
2 14-oz. jars pizza sauce
8-oz. pkg. sliced pepperoni

Alternate layers of ground beef, cooked rigatoni, cheese, soup, sauce and pepperoni in a slow cooker. Cover and cook on low setting for 4 hours.

Kitchen Tip

Slow cookers work best when filled 1/2 to 2/3 full. If they are filled to the top it is sometimes difficult to get the cooker up to temperature.

Pepperoni-Pizza Rigatoni

Penny Sherman, *Cumming, GA*

Grits with Gusto

If you like breakfast a little spicy...sprinkle warm grits with a tablespoon or two of shredded cheese and dollop a spoonful of hot salsa right in the middle.

Serves 6

2 c. long-cooking grits, uncooked
6 c. water
4-oz. can chopped green chiles
1 jalapeño pepper, seeded and finely chopped
1 t. salt
⅛ t. cayenne pepper
Optional: ½ t. paprika, ½ t. chili powder
Garnish: butter, salt and pepper

Combine all ingredients except garnish in a lightly greased slow cooker; mix well. Cover and cook on low setting for about 6 to 8 hours. Stir after first hour of cooking; stir well before serving. Serve with butter, salt and pepper.

Catherine Sedosky, *Charleston, WV*

Mom's Chili Dogs

Who can resist a good, old-fashioned chili dog?

Makes 12 servings

1 lb. lean ground beef
1 onion, chopped
½ c. catsup
6-oz. can tomato paste
2 ¼ c. water
3 T. chili powder
1 t. salt
12 hot dogs, cooked
12 hot dog buns, split

Brown ground beef until no longer pink; drain. Combine beef and remaining ingredients except hot dogs and buns; place in a slow cooker. Cover and cook for 2 to 4 hours, stirring occasionally to break up beef. To serve, spoon over hot dogs in buns.

Mom's Chili Dogs

Rogene Rogers, *Bemidji, MN*

Pork Chops à la Orange

We love these flavors together. And in the slow cooker they seem to blend even better!

Serves 6 to 8

3 lbs. pork chops
salt and pepper to taste
2 c. orange juice
2 11-oz. cans mandarin oranges, drained
8-oz. can pineapple tidbits, drained
cooked egg noodles

Sprinkle pork chops with salt and pepper; place in a slow cooker. Pour orange juice over pork. Cover and cook on low setting for 6 to 8 hours, or on high setting for 3 to 4 hours. About 30 minutes before serving, add oranges and pineapple; continue cooking just until warm. Serve with cooked noodles.

Karla Neese, *Edmond, OK*

Savory Herb Roast

My mom would always put this roast into the slow cooker early on Sunday mornings, before getting ready for church. When we came home from church around noon, the whole house smelled wonderful! Now I make it for a special weeknight dinner.

Serves 6

3-lb. boneless beef chuck roast
salt and pepper to taste
1 to 2 T. oil
1 T. fresh chives, chopped
1 T. fresh parsley, chopped
1 T. fresh basil, chopped
1 c. beef broth
**Optional: 4 to 6 potatoes, peeled and quartered;
 3 to 4 carrots, peeled and cut into chunks**

Sprinkle roast generously with salt and pepper. Heat oil in a skillet; add herbs. Brown roast on all sides. Place in slow cooker; add broth. Cover and cook on low setting for 6 to 8 hours. Add potatoes and carrots during the last 2 hours of cooking, if desired.

Savory Herb Roast

Lisa Ludwig, *Fort Wayne, IN*

Slow-Cooker Swiss Steak

Your family will love this flavorful version of an old favorite. Pick up a container of heat & eat mashed potatoes for an easy side.

Serves 4

2-lb. beef chuck roast, cut into serving-size
   pieces
3/4 c. all-purpose flour, divided
2 to 3 T. oil
16-oz. can diced tomatoes
1 onion, sliced
1 T. browning and seasoning sauce

Coat beef with 1/2 cup flour; sauté in oil in a skillet until browned. Arrange beef in a slow cooker. Combine remaining ingredients except remaining flour and pour over beef; cover and cook on low setting for 6 to 8 hours. Slowly stir in remaining flour to make gravy, adding water if necessary. Cook on high setting for 15 minutes, until thickened.

Naomi Cooper, *Delaware, OH*

Crock O' Brats

Serve with hearty rye bread and homestyle applesauce sprinkled with cinnamon.

Serves 6

20-oz. pkg. bratwurst
5 potatoes, peeled and cubed
1 tart apple, cored and cubed
1 onion, chopped
¼ c. brown sugar, packed
27-oz. can sauerkraut, drained

Brown bratwurst in a large skillet over medium heat; reserve drippings. Slice bratwurst into one-inch pieces; set aside. Combine remaining ingredients in a slow cooker. Stir in bratwurst slices with pan drippings. Cover and cook on high setting for 4 to 6 hours, or until potatoes are tender.

> ~ **Savvy Side** ~
>
> For a simple addition to this favorite slow-cooker recipe, serve with slices of French bread toasted, brushed with olive oil and sprinkled with grated cheese.

Crock O' Brats

Julie Neff, *Citrus Springs, FL*

Herb Garden Chicken

This is the chicken dish my husband asks for most often. I'm happy to oblige because it's so tasty and so easy to put together.

Makes 4 to 6 servings

4 to 6 boneless, skinless chicken breasts
2 tomatoes, chopped
1 onion, chopped
2 cloves garlic, chopped
²/₃ c. chicken broth
1 bay leaf
1 t. dried thyme
1½ t. salt
1 t. pepper, or more to taste
2 c. broccoli flowerets
Optional: 2 to 3 T. all-purpose flour
cooked rice

Place chicken in a slow cooker; top with tomatoes, onion and garlic. In a bowl, combine broth and seasonings; pour over chicken mixture. Cover and cook on low setting for 7 to 8 hours. Add broccoli; cook for one additional hour, or until chicken juices run clear and broccoli is tender. Juices in slow cooker may be thickened with flour, if desired. Discard bay leaf; serve chicken and vegetables over cooked rice.

Virginia Watson, *Scranton, PA*

New England Clam Chowder

Once you taste this, you'll never go back to canned chowder!

Serves 6

½ c. butter, melted
2 T. onion powder
2 t. dried thyme
2 stalks celery, chopped
46-oz. can clam juice
2 cubes chicken bouillon
2 bay leaves
3 16-oz. cans whole potatoes, drained and diced
3 10-oz. cans whole baby clams
2 c. light cream
2 c. milk
salt and pepper to taste

Stir together butter, onion powder, thyme and celery in a slow cooker; cover and cook on high setting for 30 minutes. Add clam juice, bouillon, bay leaves and potatoes. Cover and continue cooking on high setting for 2 hours. Add clams with juice; reduce heat to low setting. Cover and cook for 2 more hours. Stir in cream and milk; cover and cook one more hour, or until heated through. Before serving, discard bay leaves; add salt and pepper to taste.

New England Clam Chowder

Vickie, Gooseberry Patch

Thai-Style Ribs

You'll love the layers of flavor in these slow-cooker ribs. Serve with a fresh green salad for the perfect meal.

Serves 2 to 4

3$\frac{1}{2}$ lbs. pork baby back ribs, racks cut in half
11$\frac{1}{2}$-oz. can frozen orange-pineapple-apple juice concentrate, thawed
$\frac{3}{4}$ c. soy sauce
$\frac{1}{4}$ c. creamy peanut butter
$\frac{1}{4}$ c. fresh cilantro, minced
2 T. fresh ginger, peeled and minced
1 clove garlic, pressed
2 t. sugar
Garnish: fresh cilantro sprigs

Place ribs in a large shallow dish or plastic zipping bag. Whisk together remaining ingredients except garnish in a small bowl. Reserve $\frac{3}{4}$ cup mixture in refrigerator for dipping. Pour remaining mixture over ribs; cover or seal and chill 8 hours, turning occasionally. Remove ribs from marinade, discarding marinade. Place one rack of ribs in bottom of a slow cooker; stand remaining rib racks on their sides around edges of slow cooker. Cover and cook on high setting for one hour. Reduce heat to low setting; continue to cook for 5 hours. Place reserved sauce in a one-cup glass measuring cup; microwave, uncovered, on high one to 1$\frac{1}{2}$ minutes, until thoroughly heated, stirring once. Serve with ribs. Garnish with cilantro sprigs.

Lisa Wagner, Delaware, OH

Savory Pork Carnitas

Try this recipe the next time you're craving tacos or burritos. You can also enjoy it as a main dish, topped with all the garnishes.

Makes 12 servings

3-lb. Boston butt pork roast
1$\frac{1}{4}$-oz. pkg. taco seasoning mix
3 cloves garlic, sliced
1 onion, quartered
4-oz. can diced green chiles, drained
1 c. water
12 6-inch flour tortillas
Garnish: shredded lettuce, chopped tomatoes, sliced green onions, sour cream, lime wedges, fresh cilantro

Place pork roast in a slow cooker; set aside. In a bowl, combine taco seasoning mix, garlic, onion, chiles and water. Stir to combine and pour over roast. Cover and cook on low setting for 8 to 10 hours, or on high setting for 5 to 6 hours, until tender enough to shred. Spoon shredded pork down the center of tortillas. Roll up and serve with desired garnishes.

Savory Pork Carnitas

Cheryl Volbruck, *Costa Mesa, CA*

All-Day Apple Butter

A slow-cooker favorite. One taste of this apple butter on a warm biscuit or in a bowl of oatmeal and you won't be eating any other apple butter again!

Makes 5 to 6 jars

3½ lbs. Pippin apples, peeled, cored and sliced
2 lbs. Granny Smith apples, peeled, cored
and sliced
2 c. sugar
2 c. brown sugar, packed
2 t. cinnamon
¼ t. ground cloves
¼ t. salt
⅛ t. nutmeg
6 ½-pint canning jars and lids, sterilized

Place all ingredients in a large slow cooker. Stir to mix well. Cover and cook on high setting for one hour. Reduce heat to low setting and cook 9 to 11 hours more, stirring occasionally, until mixture is thick and dark brown. Uncover; cook one hour longer. Ladle hot butter into hot sterilized jars, leaving ¼-inch headspace. Wipe rims; secure with lids and rings. Process in a boiling water bath for 10 minutes. Set jars on a towel to cool; check for seals.

Amanda Fox, *South Weber, UT*

Tex-Mex Quinoa Stew

I created this slow-cooker recipe for my husband. I was determined to create something that he would love and was good for him too. Enjoy this hearty stew. My husband sure does, and he doesn't even know what quinoa is or that he's eating Greek yogurt!

Makes 8 servings

1 lb. boneless, skinless chicken breasts
14½-oz. can diced tomatoes, drained
11-oz. can corn
2 cloves garlic, minced
1 c. quinoa, uncooked
1¼-oz. pkg. salt-free taco seasoning mix
½ c. fat-free plain Greek yogurt
1 c. shredded Cheddar cheese

Place chicken in a slow cooker. Top with tomatoes, undrained corn, garlic, quinoa and taco seasoning. Cover and cook on low setting for about 7 hours, until chicken is very tender. Remove chicken to a plate. Using 2 forks, shred chicken and stir back into stew. Serve stew in bowls, topped with a dollop of plain yogurt and a sprinkle of cheese.

Tex-Mex Quinoa Stew

Heather Garthus, *Newfolden, MN*

Cajun Crockery Breakfast

This makes a great breakfast-for-dinner supper. Add a dollop of sour cream to each serving... delicious!

Makes 10 servings

32-oz. pkg. frozen diced potatoes
2 c. ground pork breakfast sausage, browned
1 c. onion, finely chopped
$\frac{1}{2}$ c. green pepper, chopped
$\frac{1}{2}$ c. mushrooms, chopped
3 c. shredded sharp Cheddar cheese
1 doz. eggs
salt, pepper and Cajun seasoning to taste
$\frac{1}{4}$ c. milk

Place half the diced potatoes in a slow cooker; top with all of the sausage and half each of the onion, green pepper, mushrooms and cheese. Repeat layering once more, ending with cheese. In a bowl, beat together eggs, seasonings and milk. Pour egg mixture over ingredients in slow cooker. Cover and cook on high setting for 4 to 6 hours, until a toothpick inserted near the center tests clean.

Brenda Smith, *Monroe, IN*

Hot Chicken Slow-Cooker Sandwiches

I like to serve these at club meetings or card parties. Everyone always asks for the recipe!

Makes 24 mini-sandwiches

28-oz. can cooked chicken
2 10 $\frac{3}{4}$-oz. cans cream of chicken soup
$\frac{1}{4}$ c. water
4 T. grated Parmesan cheese
7 slices bread, toasted and cubed
$\frac{1}{4}$ c. red pepper, chopped
24 dinner rolls, split

Combine all ingredients except rolls in a 5-quart slow cooker. Cover and cook on low setting for 3 hours. Serve on rolls.

> ⌣ **Here's a Tip** ⌣
>
> You can mix all of the ingredients for this sandwich ahead of time and keep refrigerated until ready to put in the slow cooker.

Hot Chicken Slow-Cooker
Sandwiches

Dan Ferren, *Terre Haute, IN*

Dan's Broccoli & Cheese Soup

We like to make this in our slow cooker and serve with seasoned croutons. Add a salad and you have a great meal!

Serves 6

16-oz. pkg. frozen chopped broccoli, thawed
10¾-oz. can cream of mushroom soup
1 c. milk
1 c. half-and-half
8-oz. pkg. cream cheese, cubed
1½ c. pasteurized process cheese spread, cubed
garlic powder to taste
pepper to taste

Combine all ingredients in an ungreased slow cooker; cover and cook on high setting 30 to 40 minutes. Reduce setting to low; cook an additional 3 to 4 hours, stirring occasionally.

Tammi Miller, *Attleboro, MA*

Apple Spice Country Ribs

One fall weekend after apple picking, I tossed together this recipe. I was trying to work apples into everything I could think of to use them up, and I used some of the last ones in this slow-cooker recipe. Once it was done, I wished I'd made it first so I could make it again.

Serves 6

2 to 3 lbs. boneless country pork ribs
3 baking apples, cored and cut into wedges
1 onion, thinly sliced
⅔ c. apple cider
1 t. cinnamon
1 t. allspice
½ t. salt
¼ t. pepper
Optional: mashed potatoes or cooked rice

If bone-in ribs are used, slice into serving-size portions. Place all ingredients except potatoes or rice in a 5-quart slow cooker; stir to coat. Cover and cook on low setting for 7 to 9 hours. Juices will thicken as they cool; stir if separated. Serve with mashed potatoes or hot cooked rice, if desired.

Apple Spice Country Ribs

Dana Cunningham, *Lafayette, IA*

Ham & Swiss Quiche

Who would have thought to make a yummy quiche in your slow cooker!

Serves 6

14.1-oz. pkg. refrigerated pie crusts
2 c. shredded Swiss cheese, divided
1 c. cooked ham, chopped
4 green onions, chopped
6 eggs
1 c. whipping cream
$\frac{1}{4}$ t. salt
$\frac{1}{4}$ t. pepper
$\frac{1}{8}$ t. nutmeg

Cut pie crusts in half. Press 3 pie crust halves into bottom and 2 inches up sides of a greased oval slow cooker, overlapping seams by $\frac{1}{4}$ inch. Reserve remaining pie crust half for another use. Cover and cook on high setting for $1\frac{1}{2}$ hours. Sprinkle one cup cheese, ham and green onions over crust. Whisk together eggs and remaining ingredients in a medium bowl; pour over ingredients in crust. Sprinkle remaining cheese over egg mixture. Cover and cook on high setting for $1\frac{1}{2}$ hours, or until filling is set. Uncover and let stand 5 minutes before serving. Cut quiche into wedges; serve immediately.

Carrie Knotts, *Kalispell, MT*

Easy Pork & Sauerkraut

This pork is so tender and yummy...and the side of sauerkraut cooks right with it!

Serves 6

$1\frac{1}{2}$ lb. boneless pork roast
32-oz. jar sauerkraut, undrained
12-oz. bottle regular or non-alcoholic beer
$\frac{1}{2}$ apple, peeled and cored
1 T. garlic, minced
2 t. dill weed
1 t. dry mustard

Combine all ingredients in a slow cooker; stir well. Cover and cook on high setting for one hour. Reduce to low setting and continue cooking for 5 hours, or until pork is cooked through. Discard apple before serving.

Easy Pork & Sauerkraut

Carol Lytle, *Columbus, OH*

Country Cabin Potatoes

One fall, we stayed in a beautiful 1800s log cabin in southern Ohio. Not only was it peaceful and relaxing, but the meals they served were wonderful! I got this recipe there.

Makes 10 to 12 servings

4 14 $\frac{1}{2}$-oz. cans sliced potatoes, drained
2 10 $\frac{3}{4}$-oz. cans cream of celery soup
16-oz. container sour cream
10 slices bacon, crisply cooked and crumbled
6 green onions, thinly sliced

Place potatoes in a slow cooker. In a bowl, combine remaining ingredients; pour over potatoes and stir gently. Cover and cook on high setting for 4 to 5 hours.

Mignonne Gardner, *Pleasant Grove, UT*

Slow-Cooker Steak Chili

All summer I long for cool, crisp autumn nights. I created this recipe just for those fabulous fall nights. The aroma of chili fills my home while it simmers. It makes me giddy for Halloween!

Makes 8 servings

2 lbs. beef round steak, cut into 1-inch cubes
1 $\frac{1}{2}$ c. onion, chopped
2 cloves garlic, minced
2 T. oil
1 $\frac{1}{3}$ c. water, divided
2 15-oz. cans kidney beans, drained and rinsed
2 14 $\frac{1}{2}$-oz. cans diced tomatoes
16-oz. jar salsa
15-oz. can tomato sauce
1 c. celery, chopped
1 $\frac{1}{2}$ T. chili powder
1 t. ground cumin
1 t. dried oregano
$\frac{1}{2}$ t. pepper
2 T. all-purpose flour
2 T. cornmeal
Garnish: shredded Cheddar cheese, sour cream, crushed tortilla chips

Brown beef, onion and garlic in oil in a large skillet over medium heat; drain. Add beef mixture to a 5-quart slow cooker. Stir in one cup water and remaining ingredients except flour, cornmeal and garnish; mix well. Cover and cook on low setting for 8 hours. Combine flour, cornmeal and remaining water in a small bowl, whisking until smooth. Add mixture to simmering chili right before serving; stir 2 minutes, or until thickened. Garnish as desired.

⚍ Savvy Side ⚎

Cornbread loves chili! If you like sweet cornbread, you'll love this family-size recipe. Mix together an 8-ounce box of corn muffin mix, a 9-ounce box of yellow cake mix, $\frac{1}{2}$ cup water, $\frac{1}{3}$ cup milk and 2 beaten eggs. Pour into a greased 13"x9" baking pan and bake at 350 degrees for 15 to 20 minutes. Scrumptious!

Slow-Cooker Steak Chili

Karen Hazelett, *Fremont, IN*

Slow-Cooker Pub Beer Dip

We enjoy the time we spend at Lake James in northeast Indiana. Winters at the lake are lonely for year 'rounders, so we started a monthly card club with five other couples. It's a terrific way to see your neighbors during colder months and try each other's recipes. Our friend Jan, who is a wonderful hostess, shared this slow-cooker recipe with us. It was an immediate hit!

Makes about 4 cups

2 5-oz. jars sharp Cheddar cheese spread
8-oz. pkg. cream cheese, softened
1/2 c. regular or non-alcoholic beer
1 t. Worcestershire sauce
5 to 6 drops hot pepper sauce
4 to 5 slices bacon, crisply cooked and crumbled
pretzels, crackers or sliced vegetables

Combine cheeses, beer and sauces in a greased 2 1/2 to 3-quart slow cooker. Cover and cook on low setting 2 hours, stirring occasionally; the dip will become thicker the longer it cooks. Stir in bacon just before serving, sprinkling some on top. Serve with pretzels, crackers or sliced vegetables.

Emily Martin, *Toronto, Ontario*

Beef Burgundy Stew

This classic recipe works well in a slow cooker.

Makes 10 servings

1 T. canola oil
2 lbs. stew beef cubes
4 slices bacon, crisply cooked and chopped
16-oz. pkg. frozen pearl onions, thawed
8-oz. pkg. mushrooms, quartered
6 redskin potatoes, quartered
2 carrots, peeled and cut into 1/2-inch pieces
14-oz. can beef broth
1 c. low-sodium beef broth
2 T. tomato paste
1 T. fresh thyme, snipped
1/4 t. salt
1/4 t. pepper
3 cloves garlic, minced
2 T. cornstarch
2 t. cold water

Pour oil into a stockpot. Brown beef, in batches, until browned on all sides. Combine beef, bacon and remaining ingredients except cornstarch and water in a 5-quart slow cooker. Cover and cook on low setting 7 hours or until beef and vegetables are tender. Whisk together cornstarch and water. Stir into stew. Cover and cook on high setting one hour or until slightly thickened.

Beef Burgundy Stew

Leisha Howard, *Seattle, WA*

Slow-Cooker Tapioca Pudding

When I was a child, my mom and I often made stovetop tapioca pudding and I was the stirrer. Even though both my arms would get tired, I loved helping her in the kitchen. Now that I'm older, I've mastered this slow-cooker recipe...it's just as yummy!

Serves 10 to 12

8 c. milk
1 c. small pearl tapioca, uncooked
1 to 1½ c. sugar
4 eggs, beaten
1 t. vanilla extract
½ t. almond extract
Garnish: whipped cream, sliced fresh fruit

Add milk, tapioca and sugar to a slow cooker; stir gently. Cover and cook on high setting for 3 hours. In a bowl, mix together eggs, extracts and 2 spoonfuls of hot milk mixture from slow cooker. Slowly stir mixture into slow cooker. Cover and cook on high setting for an additional 20 minutes. Chill overnight. Garnish as desired.

Lisa Sett, *Thousand Oaks, CA*

Spicy Chili Verde Soup

Just the right combination of spices makes this an all-time favorite!

Serves 8

½ lb. pork tenderloin, cut into ½-inch cubes
1 t. oil
2 c. chicken broth
2 15-oz. cans white beans, drained and rinsed
2 4-oz. cans diced green chiles
¼ t. ground cumin
¼ t. dried oregano
salt and pepper to taste
Optional: chopped fresh cilantro

Cook pork in oil in a skillet over medium heat for one to 2 minutes, until browned. Place pork in a 4-quart slow cooker. Add remaining ingredients except cilantro; stir well. Cover and cook on low setting for 4 to 6 hours. Sprinkle cilantro over each serving, if desired.

Spicy Chili Verde Soup

Lenore Mincher, *Patchogue, NY*

German Sauerbraten

Serve with spaetzle noodles tossed with butter and topped with chopped fresh parsley

Serves 12 to 14

4 to 5-lb. beef rump roast
2 t. salt
1 t. ground ginger
2½ c. water
2 c. cider vinegar
2 onions, sliced
⅓ c. sugar
2 T. pickling spice
1 t. whole peppercorns
8 whole cloves
2 bay leaves
2 T. oil
16 to 20 gingersnaps, crushed

Rub roast all over with salt and ginger; place in a deep glass bowl and set aside. Combine water, vinegar, onions, sugar and spices in a saucepan; bring to a boil. Pour over roast; turn to coat. Cover roast and refrigerate for 3 days, turning twice each day. Remove roast, reserving marinade; pat dry. Heat oil in a Dutch oven; brown roast on all sides. Place roast in a slow cooker. Strain marinade, reserving half of onions and spices. Pour 1½ cups marinade, onions and spices over roast; refrigerate remaining marinade. Cover and cook on low setting for 6 to 7 hours, until roast is tender. Remove roast to a platter; keep warm. Discard onions and spices; add enough of refrigerated marinade to liquid from slow cooker to equal 3½ cups. Pour into a saucepan; bring to a boil. Add crushed gingersnaps; simmer until gravy thickens. Slice roast; serve with gravy.

Jennifer Martineau, *Delaware, OH*

Gramma's Smothered Swiss Steak

These little nuggets of beef are so rich and yummy. Serve with fresh green beans and new potatoes.

Serves 6

1½ lbs. beef round steak, cut into
    serving-size pieces
1 T. oil
1 small onion, halved and sliced
1 carrot, peeled and shredded
1 c. sliced mushrooms
10¾-oz. can cream of chicken soup
8-oz. can tomato sauce
½ c. water

Brown beef in oil in a skillet over medium heat; drain and set aside. Arrange vegetables in a slow cooker; place beef on top. Mix together soup and tomato sauce; pour over beef and vegetables. Cover and cook on low setting for 6 hours, or until beef is tender.

Gramma's Smothered Swiss Steak

Pat Beach, *Fisherville, KY*

Slow-Cooked Veggie Beef Soup

What could be easier than this old-fashioned beef soup?

Makes 12 servings

1½ lbs. stew beef cubes
46-oz. can cocktail vegetable juice
2 c. water
5 cubes beef bouillon
½ onion, chopped
3 potatoes, peeled and cubed
3 c. cabbage, shredded
16-oz. pkg. frozen mixed vegetables

Place all ingredients in a slow cooker. Cover and cook on low setting for 9 hours, or until all ingredients are tender.

Angela Couillard, *Lakeville, MN*

Sausage-Stuffed Squash

These are so pretty on each individual plate. Everyone will love them!

Makes 4 servings

12-oz. pkg. smoked turkey sausage, diced
⅓ c. dark brown sugar, packed
¼ t. dried sage
2 acorn squash, halved and seeded
1 c. water

In a bowl, mix together sausage, brown sugar and sage; toss to mix well. Fill squash halves heaping full with sausage mixture; wrap each stuffed half with aluminum foil. Pour water into a large slow cooker; place wrapped squash halves in slow cooker, stacking if necessary. Cover and cook on low setting for 6 to 8 hours.

Sausage-Stuffed Squash

Gretchen Hickman, *Galva, IL*

Crockery Apple Pie

I received this recipe from my great-aunt who owned an orchard. This smells heavenly when it's cooking, and it's perfect served with a scoop of vanilla bean ice cream.

Makes 12 servings

8 tart apples, peeled, cored and sliced
2 t. cinnamon
¼ t. allspice
¼ t. nutmeg
1 c. milk
2 T. butter, softened
¾ c. sugar
2 eggs, beaten
1 t. vanilla extract
1 ½ c. biscuit baking mix, divided
⅓ c. brown sugar, packed
3 T. chilled butter

In a large bowl, toss apples with spices. Spoon apple mixture into a lightly greased slow cooker. In separate bowl, combine milk, softened butter, sugar, eggs, vanilla and ½ cup baking mix; stir until well mixed. Spoon batter over apples. Place remaining baking mix and brown sugar in small bowl. Cut in chilled butter until coarse crumbs form. Sprinkle over batter in slow cooker. Cover and cook on low setting for 6 to 7 hours.

Barbara Burke, *Newport News, VA*

The Easiest Rice Pudding

We love old-fashioned rice pudding, and this version made in the slow cooker is so simple!

Makes 10 servings

8 c. whole milk
1 c. long-cooking brown rice, uncooked
½ c. sugar
3 eggs
¼ c. light cream
¾ c. dried cranberries
2 t. vanilla extract
½ t. cinnamon
¼ t. salt

Spray a slow cooker with non-stick vegetable spray; set aside. In a bowl, combine milk, uncooked rice and sugar; mix well. Spoon milk mixture into slow cooker. Cover and cook on low setting for 5 hours, or until rice is tender. When rice is tender, beat together eggs, cream and remaining ingredients. Whisk ½ cup of milk mixture from slow cooker into egg mixture. Continue whisking in the milk mixture, ½ cup at a time, until only half remains in slow cooker. Spoon everything back into slow cooker; stir. Cover and cook on low setting for one hour.

The Easiest Rice Pudding

Blender Recipes

The blender that sits on your counter, always ready to help, is no doubt a favorite appliance. This kitchen friend has been around for years and continues to step up every time you need a smooth texture in a jiffy. You'll love the assortment of blender recipes we offer in the chapter including favorite drinks like an Autumn Apple Milkshake or Raspberry Cream Smoothies. The soups we share will become some of your favorites. Our Creamy Asparagus Soup is as beautiful as it is yummy and our October Bisque is rich and creamy. Your blender is also a great way to make creamy dips and full-of-flavor pestos like Olive Pesto and Chickpea & Red Pepper Dip. So bring that blender back into action with some fresh recipes that your family & friends are sure to enjoy.

Vickie, *Gooseberry Patch*

Watermelon Fruitsicles

Everyone loves a cool summer treat!

Makes one dozen

5-1b. watermelon, seeded and cubed
½ c. sugar
1 env. unflavored gelatin
1 T. lemon juice

Place half of watermelon in container of an electric blender; process until smooth. Repeat procedure with remaining watermelon. Strain watermelon purée into a large measuring cup, discarding pulp. Reserve 4 cups watermelon juice. Combine one cup juice and sugar in a saucepan. Sprinkle gelatin over mixture; let stand one minute. Cook over medium heat, stirring constantly, until sugar and gelatin dissolve. Add gelatin mixture to remaining 3 cups watermelon juice; stir in lemon juice and let cool. Pour into ⅓-cup frozen pop molds; freeze.

Stacie Avner, *Delaware, OH*

Freezy Fruit Pops

Both kids and adults will love these freezer pops made with fresh fruit. Invent new flavors using other favorite soft fruits!

Makes 2 dozen

½ c. sugar
2 c. boiling water
20-oz. can crushed pineapple
10-oz. pkg. frozen strawberries, thawed
6-oz. can frozen orange juice concentrate, thawed
5 ripe bananas, mashed
24 3-oz. paper cups
24 wooden craft sticks

In a bowl, dissolve sugar in boiling water. Stir in pineapple with juice and remaining ingredients. In 2 batches, pour mixture into a blender; process until smooth. Ladle into paper cups; set in a pan. Freeze until partially frozen; insert a stick in each cup. Return to freezer until frozen. To serve, peel away cup.

Patricia Reitz, *Winchester, VA*

Blueberry Flaxseed Smoothies

This smoothie will be a good start to your day.

Serves 4

1 banana, cut into chunks
½ c. blueberries
1 c. low-fat vanilla yogurt
1 c. fat-free milk
2 T. ground flaxseed
Garnish: fresh strawberries, blueberries, flaxseed

Combine all ingredients except garnish in a blender; process on high setting until smooth. Pour into glasses. Garnish with fruit and flaxseed.

Blueberry Flaxseed Smoothies

Dawn Henning, *Delaware, OH*

Greek Chicken & Rice Soup

When you serve a rotisserie chicken with rice for supper, reserve some to enjoy in soup for the next night. Pita bread and tomatoes pair well with this soup.

Serves 4

4 c. chicken broth
2 c. cooked rice, divided
2 egg yolks, beaten
1 T. lemon zest
3 T. lemon juice
1 to 2 c. deli roast chicken, shredded
salt and pepper to taste
Optional: 2 T. fresh dill or parsley, chopped
Garnish: sliced black olives, lemon slices

Bring broth to a simmer in a large saucepan over medium heat. Transfer one cup hot broth to a blender. Add ½ cup cooked rice, egg yolks, lemon zest and juice to blender; cover and blend until smooth. Stir rice mixture into simmering broth; add chicken and remaining rice. Simmer, stirring frequently, about 10 minutes, until slightly thickened. Add salt and pepper to taste. At serving time, stir in dill or parsley, and garnish as desired.

Shirl Parsons, *Cape Carteret, NC*

Raspberry Cream Smoothies

I have been making these refreshing smoothies for years. They're a delicious treat for any time of day!

Makes 8 servings

3 c. frozen raspberries
1 c. banana, cubed and frozen
2 c. orange juice
2 c. frozen vanilla yogurt
2 c. raspberry yogurt
2 t. vanilla extract

In a blender, combine frozen fruit and remaining ingredients. Process until smooth; stir, if needed. Pour into chilled glasses.

Vickie, *Gooseberry Patch*

Banana-Mango Soy Smoothies

So quick to make and so good for you!

Serves 6

2 c. vanilla or plain soy milk
2 to 3 bananas, sliced and frozen
6 mangoes, pitted, peeled, cubed and frozen
1 T. honey, or to taste

Combine all ingredients in a blender. Blend on high setting until smooth and frothy. Pour into tall glasses.

Raspberry Cream Smoothies

Jo Ann, *Gooseberry Patch*

Peppermint Milkshakes

This yummy dessert drink appeals to all ages. Use less milk for really thick shakes.

Makes 9¼ cups

8 c. vanilla ice cream, divided
2 c. milk, divided
1 c. hard peppermint round candies (about 40 to 50 candies), crushed and divided
8½-oz. can refrigerated instant whipped cream
Garnish: peppermint sticks

Process 4 cups ice cream, one cup milk and ½ cup crushed candies in a blender until smooth, stopping to scrape down sides as needed. Pour into small serving glasses; top with whipped cream and place a peppermint stick in each glass. Repeat with remaining ingredients.
Note: Process peppermint candies in a food processor for quick crushing.

Julie Dossantos, *Fort Pierce, FL*

Sunshine State Smoothies

This smoothie combines the citrus goodness from our home state of Florida with other healthful fruits and veggies.

Serves 2

4 to 5 ice cubes
1 peach, halved, pitted and cubed
4-oz. container low-fat peach or vanilla yogurt
1 to 2 bananas, sliced
¼ c. orange juice
10 baby carrots
Optional: orange or peach slices

Combine all ingredients except optional garnish in a blender. Process well for about one minute. Pour into 2 glasses; garnish with fruit slices, if desired.

Marsha Overholser, *Ash Grove, MO*

Nutty Banana Shake

A tasty way to use ripe bananas. Bananas will ripen quickly if placed overnight in a brown paper bag.

Serves one

2 to 3 bananas, peeled and frozen
1 c. milk
2 T. peanut butter
1 T. honey

Slice frozen bananas and place in a blender with remaining ingredients. Blend until smooth and thick. Serve immediately.

Nutty Banana Shake

Vickie, *Gooseberry Patch*

Autumn Apple Milkshake

This cool treat really hits the spot after a long session of raking leaves!

Serves 6

14-oz. can sweetened condensed milk
1 c. applesauce
½ c. apple cider
½ t. apple pie spice
3 c. crushed ice
Garnish: cinnamon

In a blender, combine all ingredients except ice and cinnamon. Gradually add ice, blending until smooth. Garnish with cinnamon.

Paulette Alexander, *Newfoundland, Canada*

Chickpea & Red Pepper Dip

This is always a favorite dip at our family get-togethers.

Makes 8 servings, or about 2 cups

19-oz. can garbanzo beans, drained and rinsed
12-oz. jar roasted red peppers, drained and sliced
½ c. sour cream
1 to 2 cloves garlic, chopped
½ t. red pepper flakes
¼ t. salt
¼ t. pepper

Combine all ingredients in a food processor or blender. Process until smooth; transfer to a serving dish.

⌐ Here's a Tip ⌐

Clean your blender in a jiffy! Fill halfway with hot water and add a drop of dish soap. Holding a towel on the lid, process for about 10 seconds. Pour out the soapy water and rinse with fresh water...done!

Chickpea & Red Pepper Dip

Pat Minnich, *El Cajon, CA*

Creamy Basil Salad Dressing

I grow my own basil and love this recipe. The dressing is so flavorful you would never guess it's low in fat!

Makes about 1½ cups

1 t. shallot, chopped
1 clove garlic, chopped
⅔ c. Greek yogurt
3 T. balsamic vinegar
1 T. lemon juice
3 T. olive oil
½ c. fresh basil, finely chopped
salt and pepper to taste

Place all ingredients except salt and pepper in a food processor or blender. Process until smooth. Season with salt and pepper. Keep refrigerated.

Colleen Hinker, *Santa Rosa, NM*

Fresh Herb Pesto Sauce

Classic pesto is made with basil and pine nuts, but you can try other tasty combinations like rosemary and pecans or oregano and almonds...delicious!

Makes about 1½ cups

2 c. fresh herb leaves, coarsely chopped
6 cloves garlic, chopped
1 c. nuts, chopped
½ c. olive oil
½ t. salt
¾ c. grated Parmesan or Romano cheese

Mix herbs, garlic, nuts, oil and salt in a blender. Process until smooth, adding a little more oil if needed to make blending easier. Transfer to a bowl and stir in grated cheese. Refrigerate in an airtight container.

~ **Kitchen Tip** ~

Freeze pesto in ice cube trays to have it ready to add to soups, stews and casseroles.

Fresh Herb Pesto Sauce

Julie Dossantos, *Fort Pierce, FL*

Autumn Morning Smoothie

Our family loves to make breakfast smoothies. After baking pie pumpkins, I decided to try making smoothies for Thanksgiving morning. I served them in bowls instead of glasses for a fun change of pace.

Makes 2 servings

½ c. fresh pumpkin purée or canned pumpkin
¾ c. papaya, peeled, seeded and cubed
2 bananas, sliced
½ c. low-fat vanilla yogurt
¼ c. orange juice
4 ice cubes
1½ t. cinnamon
Garnish: additional cinnamon

Add all ingredients except garnish to a blender. Process until smooth; pour into 2 tall glasses or bowls. Top each with a sprinkle of cinnamon.

Lisa McClelland, *Columbus, OH*

Cucumber-Lime Agua Fresca

On a trip to Mexico, I was served this beverage one hot day. It's very refreshing...a great way to use up cucumbers and mint! The lime adds the tartness.

Makes 4 servings

1 lb. cucumbers, cubed
6 c. water, divided
¼ c. fresh mint, chopped
2 T. sugar
2 T. lime juice
ice cubes
Garnish: lime slices, cucumber slices

Combine cucumbers, 2 cups water and mint in a blender. Process until puréed. Let stand in blender for 5 minutes to steep. Strain purée into a 2-quart pitcher. Add remaining water, sugar, lime juice and ice. Stir to combine; add more sugar, if desired. Divide evenly into 4 tall glasses; garnish as desired. Serve immediately.

Cucumber-Lime Agua Fresca

Jessica Phillips, *Santa Clarita, CA*

Just Peachy Coconut Smoothies

Try fresh peaches in this recipe if you have some...yummy!

Serves 2

16-oz. pkg. frozen peaches, divided
14-oz. can coconut milk
2 T. unsweetened flaked coconut
1 T. honey
1 t. vanilla extract

Place half the peaches in a blender; reserve remaining peaches for another recipe. Add remaining ingredients to blender; process mixture until smooth and creamy, about 30 seconds. If consistency is too thin, add a few extra frozen peaches to thicken.

Patricia Walker, *Mocksville, NC*

Supreme Cheesecake Dip

Make the serving bowl for this dip kid-friendly and fun.

Makes about 3 cups

2 8-oz. pkgs. cream cheese, softened
½ c. frozen strawberries, thawed and drained
¼ c. sugar
¼ c. sour cream
1½ t. vanilla extract
graham crackers, fresh fruit

Combine cream cheese, strawberries, sugar, sour cream and vanilla in a blender. Cover and blend until very smooth; chill at least 2 hours. Serve with graham crackers and fresh fruit for dipping.

Etha Hutchcroft, *Ames, IA*

Strawberry Preserves Smoothies

We love to make these smoothies for a quick snack or even for a drink at dinnertime. We like strawberries so much that we choose that flavor, but you can use raspberries or any other fruit you like.

Makes 4 servings

2 T. strawberry preserves
1 c. crushed pineapple
1 c. orange juice
3 c. fresh strawberries, hulled and sliced
8-oz. container low-fat strawberry yogurt
8-oz. container low-fat plain yogurt

Combine all ingredients in a blender; process until smooth. Pour into chilled jelly jars to serve.

Strawberry Preserves Smoothies

Mary Murray, *Mount Vernon, OH*

October Bisque

Even though I call this "October Bisque" it is good any month of the year.

Makes 8 servings

1 onion, chopped
¼ c. butter
4 c. chicken broth
28-oz. can whole tomatoes
1 T. sugar
2 15-oz. cans pumpkin
2 T. fresh parsley, chopped
2 T. fresh chives, chopped

Sauté onion in butter until onion is tender. Add broth and simmer for 15 minutes. Place tomatoes with juice in a blender or food processor and blend until smooth. Add tomato mixture, sugar, pumpkin, parsley and chives to broth; heat through.

Elaine Slabinski, *Monroe Township, NJ*

Creamy Asparagus Soup

This soup is so beautiful! Top with freshly steamed asparagus tips for the perfect garnish.

Makes 4 servings

1½ lbs. asparagus, trimmed and chopped
14½-oz. can chicken broth
1 T. onion, minced
¼ t. salt
¼ t. white pepper
½ c. milk

Set aside a few asparagus tips for garnish. Combine remaining ingredients except milk in a soup pot over medium heat. Bring to a boil; reduce heat and simmer 5 to 7 minutes, or until asparagus is tender. Working in small batches, ladle asparagus mixture into a blender. Add milk slowly and purée. Return mixture to soup pot and heat through without boiling. Steam or microwave reserved asparagus tips just until tender; use to garnish soup.

Creamy Asparagus Soup

Amy Butcher, *Columbus, GA*

Old-Fashioned Ginger Beer

I make this for picnics in the summertime and it has become a drink everyone looks forward to.

Serves 10

4 lemons
1 orange
¾ c. fresh ginger, peeled and coarsely chopped
¾ c. sugar
¾ c. honey
2 c. boiling water
1¼ c. orange juice
4 c. sparkling mineral water, chilled
crushed ice
Garnish: orange slices

Grate 2 tablespoons of zest from one lemon and one orange. Set zest aside. Refrigerate lemon and orange for slices later. Squeeze ⅓ cup lemon juice from remaining 3 lemons. Set juice aside. Pulse ginger, sugar and honey in a blender just until combined; spoon into a pitcher. Add orange and lemon zests, lemon juice and boiling water; stir until sugar dissolves. Cool to room temperature. Stir in orange juice. Cover and refrigerate for at least 24 hours and up to 4 days. Strain before serving. Thinly slice refrigerated lemon and orange; add to pitcher. Stir in sparkling water. Serve over ice. Garnish as desired.

Vickie, *Gooseberry Patch*

Butternut Squash Soup

A creamy, flavorful soup that is perfect to start a holiday meal.

Makes 8 cups

3-lb. butternut squash
8 carrots, peeled and cut into pieces
2½ c. chicken broth
¾ c. orange juice
½ t. salt
½ t. ground ginger
½ c. whipping cream
Garnish: sour cream, finely chopped toasted
    pecans, nutmeg

Cut squash in half lengthwise; remove seeds. Place squash, cut-sides down, in a shallow pan; add hot water to pan to a depth of ¾ inch. Cover with aluminum foil and bake at 400 degrees for 40 minutes or until tender; drain. Scoop out pulp; mash. Discard shell. Cook carrots in boiling water 25 minutes or until tender; drain and mash. Combine squash, carrots, chicken broth and next 3 ingredients in a bowl. Process half of mixture in a food processor or blender until smooth. Repeat procedure with remaining half of squash mixture. Place puréed mixture in a large saucepan; bring to a simmer. Stir in cream; return to a simmer. Remove from heat. Ladle into bowls and garnish as desired.

Butternut Squash Soup

Gretchen Ham, *Pine City, NY*

Quick & Easy Tomato Soup

Fresh basil really makes this soup special. The flavors get even better when it is warmed up the next day!

Makes 10 servings

½ c. butter, sliced
1 c. fresh basil, chopped
2 28-oz. cans crushed tomatoes
2 cloves garlic, minced
1 qt. half-and-half
salt and pepper to taste
Garnish: fresh parsley, sliced cherry
 tomatoes, croutons

In a large saucepan, melt butter over medium heat. Add basil; sauté for 2 minutes. Add tomatoes with juice and garlic; reduce heat and simmer for 20 minutes. Remove from heat; let cool slightly. Working in batches, transfer tomato mixture to a blender and purée. Strain into a separate saucepan and add half-and-half, mixing very well. Reheat soup over medium-low heat; add salt and pepper to taste. Garnish as desired.

Louise McGaha, *Clinton, TN*

Traditional Hummus

I love this recipe...it's just right for a snack or a quick lunch.

Makes 2 cups, serves 10

2 15-oz. cans garbanzo beans, drained and
 rinsed
½ c. warm water
3 T. lime or lemon juice
1 T. tahini sesame seed paste
1½ t. ground cumin
1 T. garlic, minced
¼ t. salt

Place all ingredients in a food processor or blender. Process until very smooth, about 4 minutes. If a thinner consistency is desired, add an extra tablespoon or 2 of water. Transfer to a serving bowl.

Traditional Hummus

Cheri Maxwell, *Gulf Breeze, FL*

Break-of-Day Smoothie

Make this just the way you like it, using your favorite flavors of yogurt and fruit.

Serves 2

15¼-oz. can fruit cocktail
8-oz. container vanilla yogurt
1 c. pineapple juice
6 to 8 ice cubes
Optional: 3 to 4 T. wheat germ

Combine all ingredients in a blender. Blend until smooth. Pour into tall glasses and serve.

Michelle Powell, *Valley, AL*

Spicy Broccomole

A delicious, creamy dip or topping for tacos, burritos and quesadillas that is low-cal and low-fat. For an extra-spicy flavor, leave in some of the jalapeño seeds.

Makes 3 cups, serves 8

3 c. fresh or frozen broccoli flowerets
1 jalapeño pepper, roasted, seeded and chopped
1 green onion, chopped
⅓ c. plain Greek yogurt
3 T. fresh cilantro, chopped
1 t. olive oil
¼ t. chili powder
¼ t. garlic powder
¼ t. salt
¼ t. pepper

In a saucepan over medium-high heat, cook broccoli in salted water until very soft. Drain well, squeezing out water with a paper towel. Transfer broccoli to a food processor or blender; add remaining ingredients. Process until smooth. If a smoother texture is desired, add a little more olive oil. Serve warm.

Spicy Broccomole

Jen Stout, *Blandon, PA*

Fajita & Bowties Salad Bowl

*Try Cheddar or ranch-flavored tortilla chips...
they add extra flavor to this salad!*

Makes 4 servings

¼ c. lime juice
1 T. ground cumin
½ t. chili powder
½ c. fresh cilantro, chopped
½ c. olive oil
15-oz. can black beans, drained and rinsed
11-oz. can corn, drained
1 c. salsa
2 tomatoes, chopped
8-oz. pkg. bowtie pasta, cooked
2 c. tortilla chips, crushed
1 c. shredded Cheddar cheese

Combine lime juice and spices in a food processor
or blender. Process until almost smooth; drizzle in
oil and process until blended. Set aside. In a large
bowl combine beans, corn, salsa, tomatoes, pasta
and lime juice mixture; toss to combine. Gently
mix in tortilla chips and cheese. Cover and chill
until serving time.

Katie Majeske, *Denver, PA*

Island Chiller

Such a refreshing drink on a hot summer day.

Makes 8 servings

10-oz. pkg. frozen strawberries
15-oz. can crushed pineapple
1½ c. orange juice
1-qt. bottle club soda or sparkling water, chilled
Optional: strawberries

In a blender, combine frozen strawberries,
pineapple with juice and orange juice. Blend until
smooth and frothy. Pour mixture into ice cube
trays and freeze. To serve, put 3 cubes into each
of 8 tall glasses; add ½ cup club soda or sparkling
water to each glass. Let stand until mixture
becomes slushy. Garnish each glass with a
strawberry, if desired.

Island Chiller

Marcia Marcoux, *Charlton, MA*

Creamy Raspberry Mousse

It's a snap to make this elegant and delicious dessert.

Makes 6 servings

1½ c. white chocolate chips
1 c. milk
12-oz. pkg. frozen raspberries, thawed
2 to 3 T. sugar
2 3.9-oz. pkgs. instant white chocolate
    pudding mix
2 c. frozen whipped topping, thawed
Optional: ½ c. chopped pistachios

Combine white chocolate chips and milk in a large microwave-safe bowl. Microwave mixture on high 15 seconds at a time, stirring between each interval, until chips are melted. Place in refrigerator until cold; stir occasionally to minimize separation. Process raspberries and sugar in a blender until smooth. Strain seeds, if desired; set aside. When chocolate mixture is cold, add pudding mix. Beat with an electric mixer at medium speed for 2 minutes. Fold in whipped topping; refrigerate at least one hour. Divide among 6 individual serving bowls; top each with about 2 tablespoons of raspberry mixture. Sprinkle with pistachios, if desired.

April Haury, *Paramus, NJ*

Mom's Best Fruit Smoothies

This simple smoothie is one of our family favorites...and so easy!

Makes 3 servings

1½ c. fresh or frozen peaches, cut into chunks
2 mangoes, pitted and diced
1 banana, cut into chunks
8-oz. container non-fat plain yogurt
1 T. honey

Combine fruit, yogurt and honey in a blender. Process until smooth; pour into tall glasses.

Sandy Benhan, *Sanborn, NY*

Strawberry-Watermelon Slush

A luscious combination of fresh summer fruit.

Serves 5 to 6

1 pt. strawberries, hulled and halved
2 c. watermelon, cubed and seeded
⅓ c. sugar
⅓ c. lemon juice
2 c. ice cubes

Combine all ingredients except ice cubes in a blender. Process until smooth. Gradually add ice and continue to blend. Serve immediately.

Mom's Best Fruit Smoothies

Jen Stout, *Blandon, PA*

Olive Pesto

This unusual pesto will become a favorite!

Makes one cup

¾ c. pitted Kalamata or ripe olives
½ c. fresh flat-leaf parsley sprigs, packed
¼ c. fresh basil leaves, packed
1 shallot, chopped
2 cloves garlic, pressed
3 T. extra-virgin olive oil
¼ c. grated Parmesan cheese

Process first 5 ingredients in a blender until minced, stopping to scrape down sides. Add oil and cheese; process until blended. Transfer to a small bowl. Cover and chill, if desired. Store in refrigerator.

Angela Murphy, *Tempe, AZ*

Very Berry Vinaigrette

A can't-miss dressing that's yummy on spinach salad.

Makes about 2½ cups

¼ c. olive oil
1 c. seasoned rice vinegar
10-oz. jar seedless raspberry jam

Combine all ingredients in a blender; blend until smooth. Cover and refrigerate until ready to serve.

Tina Butler, *Royce City, TX*

Fresh Spinach Smoothie

The fresh spinach in this smoothie gives it an amazingly beautiful color and the touch of honey gives it a sweet taste.

Makes 3 servings

1 c. skim milk
2 bananas, sliced and frozen
1½ c. fresh spinach, torn into pieces, stems removed
¾ c. ice
1 T. honey

Combine milk, bananas, spinach, ice and honey in a blender; process on high setting until smooth. Pour into glasses to serve.

Fresh Spinach Smoothie

Waffle Iron Recipes

You and your family enjoy those deliciously classic waffles that come piping-hot from your trusty waffle iron...Yummy Blueberry Waffles, Nutty Maple Waffles and Cocoa Waffles. Whether you like syrup, jelly, or butter on top, everyone loves them all! But this favorite appliance can also be used to make other goodies like Grandmother's Waffle Cookies, Chocolate Waffle Ice Cream Treats, savory Corn Waffle Tostadas and Herb Waffles. Need a quick sandwich to serve on short notice? Let your waffle iron help you make sandwiches like Quick English Muffin Sandwiches or Special Waffle Sandwiches in a jiffy. So take a fresh look at this much-loved appliance and create some tried & true, fresh and new recipes that come straight from your waffle iron to your table, bringing smiles to everyone.

Jo Ann, *Gooseberry Patch*

Cocoa Waffles

Serve these chocolatey waffles with hot maple syrup and a dollop of sweetened whipped cream.

Makes 8 waffles

2 eggs, beaten
3/4 c. whipping cream
1 1/4 c. cake flour
1/2 t. salt
3 t. baking powder
6 T. baking cocoa
1/2 c. sugar
1/4 c. butter, melted
1/4 t. vanilla extract
2 egg whites

Blend eggs and cream. Sift together dry ingredients; stir into egg mixture. Add butter and vanilla; mix well. In a separate bowl, beat egg whites on high speed until stiff peaks form; fold into batter. Bake in waffle iron 1 1/2 to 2 minutes or until crispy.

Jennifer Bontrager, *Oklahoma City, OK*

Yummy Blueberry Waffles

Our whole family loves these waffles. I can't make them fast enough...I keep them warm in the oven so I can sit down and enjoy them too!

Makes 4 waffles

2 eggs
2 c. all-purpose flour
1 3/4 c. milk
1/2 c. oil
1 T. sugar
4 t. baking powder
1/4 t. salt
1/2 t. vanilla extract
1 to 1 1/2 c. blueberries
Optional: chopped pecans

In a large bowl, beat eggs with an electric mixer on medium speed until fluffy. Add remaining ingredients except blueberries and pecans if using; beat just until smooth. Spray a waffle iron with non-stick vegetable spray. Pour batter by 1/2 cupfuls onto the preheated waffle iron. Scatter desired amount of blueberries over batter. Bake according to manufacturer's directions, until golden. Serve with chopped pecans on top, if desired.

Yummy Blueberry Waffles

Kathy Grashoff, *Fort Wayne, IN*

Whipping Cream Waffles & Cranberry Butter

I just love waffles on a snowy morning with nowhere to rush off to!

Makes 2 servings

8-oz. container whipping cream
2 eggs, separated
1 T. butter, melted and slightly cooled
2/3 c. all-purpose flour
1/3 c. sugar
1 t. baking powder
1/8 t. salt

In a deep bowl, beat cream with an electric mixer on medium speed until soft peaks form. In a separate bowl, beat egg yolks with a fork until thick and light-colored; fold in whipped cream and butter. Combine flour, sugar, baking powder and salt in a small bowl. Fold into whipped cream mixture. Beat egg whites on high speed until stiff peaks form; fold into batter. Batter will be thick. For each waffle, spoon half of batter onto a preheated, oiled waffle iron, spreading to edges. Bake according to manufacturer's directions, until crisp and lightly golden. Serve with Cranberry Butter.

CRANBERRY BUTTER:

1/2 c. butter, softened
1/4 c. powdered sugar
2 T. whole-berry cranberry sauce

Combine butter and powdered sugar; beat with an electric mixer on medium speed until blended. Stir in cranberry sauce; chill.

Shannon Sitko, *Warren, OH*

Grandmother's Waffle Cookies

My Grandmother Blanche always made these delicious cookies...we loved them!

Makes 3 dozen

1 c. butter, melted and slightly cooled
4 eggs, beaten
1 c. sugar
1 c. brown sugar, packed
2 t. vanilla extract
4 c. all-purpose flour
Optional: frosting and sprinkles

Mix together melted butter, eggs and sugars; add vanilla. Slowly stir in flour. Drop batter by teaspoonfuls onto a preheated ungreased waffle iron. Check cookies after about one minute. Cookies are done when they are a medium golden in center and light golden at the edges. Dip in frosting and sprinkles, if desired.

Grandmother's Waffle Cookies

Angela Murphy, *Tempe, AZ*

Corn Waffle Tostadas

My whole family loves this new way to enjoy Mexican tostadas.

Serves 6

1 lb. lean ground beef
¾ c. water
1-oz. pkg. taco seasoning mix
8½-oz. pkg. corn muffin mix
½ c. milk
1 egg, beaten
2 T. shortening, melted
Garnish: shredded lettuce, shredded Cheddar
  cheese, diced tomatoes, sliced green onions,
  sour cream

Brown beef in a skillet over medium heat. Drain; stir in water and taco seasoning. Meanwhile, beat together corn muffin mix, milk, egg and shortening. Add ¾ cup batter per waffle to a preheated, greased waffle iron. Bake according to manufacturer's directions. Top waffles with beef mixture; garnish as desired.

Rita Morgan, *Pueblo, CO*

Jelly French Toast

Jazz up everyday French toast in a jiffy with a spoonful of your favorite jelly or jam tucked between two slices of bread.

Makes 6 sandwiches

12 slices bread
¾ c. favorite flavor jam or jelly
3 eggs, beaten
½ c. milk
1 t. sugar
¼ t. salt
¼ c. butter, softened

Assemble 6 sandwiches using bread and jelly or jam; set aside. Whisk together eggs, milk, sugar and salt in a shallow bowl. Dip each sandwich into egg mixture. Cook one sandwich at a time on a preheated, buttered waffle iron, about 5 minutes per side, until crisp and golden.

⁓ **Change it up** ⁓

For the perfect cousin to a PB & J, add a tablespoon of peanut butter with the jelly when you make this yummy French toast.

Jelly French Toast

Diana Chaney, *Olathe, KS*

Spicy-Sweet Corn Waffles

Something different for breakfast or brunch! Or cut into "fingers" for dipping into chili.

Makes 6 servings

3 canned chipotle peppers in adobo sauce
¾ c. milk
2 c. biscuit baking mix
14¾-oz. can cream-style corn
2 T. oil
1 egg, beaten
Optional: maple syrup

Combine peppers and milk in a blender. Process until smooth; set aside. Mix remaining ingredients except syrup in a large bowl; add pepper mixture. Stir until combined. For each waffle, add ¾ cup batter to a preheated, greased waffle iron. Bake according to manufacturer's directions, until crisp and golden. Serve with maple syrup, if desired.

Vickie, *Gooseberry Patch*

Nutty Maple Waffles

Crunchy pecans paired with maple...a great way to begin the day! Top with plenty of butter and rich maple syrup.

Serves 8

1½ c. all-purpose flour
2 T. sugar
1 t. baking powder
¼ t. salt
2 eggs, separated
12-oz. can evaporated milk
3 T. oil
½ t. maple extract
Optional: finely chopped pecans

Combine flour, sugar, baking powder and salt in a medium bowl; mix well and set aside. Combine egg yolks, evaporated milk, oil and maple extract in a large bowl; blend well. Gradually add flour mixture, beating well after each addition; set aside. Beat egg whites in a small bowl at high speed with an electric mixer until stiff peaks form; fold into batter. For each waffle, pour about ½ cup batter onto a preheated, greased waffle iron; sprinkle with pecans if desired. Cook according to manufacturer's instructions.

Nutty Maple Waffles

Tamara Ahrens, *Sparta, MI*

Mom's Everything Waffles

The delicious flavors of peanut butter, pecans, blueberries and even chocolate come together in this one-of-a-kind breakfast favorite.

Serves 4 to 6

2 c. biscuit baking mix
1½ c. quick-cooking oats, uncooked
¼ c. wheat germ
½ c. chopped pecans or walnuts
2 eggs, beaten
¼ c. peanut butter
½ c. vanilla yogurt
3½ c. milk, divided
1 c. blueberries
Optional: ¼ c. mini chocolate chips
Garnish: maple syrup, fruit topping, whipped
   cream

Combine baking mix, oats, wheat germ and nuts in a large bowl; set aside. In a separate bowl, whisk together eggs, peanut butter, yogurt and 3 cups milk. Add to dry ingredients and stir. Add remaining milk as needed to get the consistency of applesauce. Fold in blueberries and chocolate chips, if desired. Pour by ½ cupfuls onto a preheated waffle iron that has been sprayed with non-stick vegetable spray. Bake until crisp, according to manufacturer's directions. Serve with maple syrup, fruit topping or a dollop of whipped cream.

Lisa McClelland, *Columbus, OH*

Oatmeal Waffles

These waffles were a favorite holiday breakfast of mine when I was growing up. They are wholesome and yummy, especially when topped with fresh berries.

Makes 10 waffles, serves 10

1½ c. all-purpose flour
1 c. quick-cooking rolled oats, uncooked
1 T. baking powder
¼ t. sea salt
2 t. pumpkin pie spice
1 t. vanilla extract
2 eggs, lightly beaten
1½ c. milk
4 T. butter, melted and slightly cooled
2 T. brown sugar, packed
Garnish: fresh raspberries, warmed
   maple syrup

In a large bowl, mix together flour, oats, baking powder, salt, spice and vanilla; set aside. In a separate bowl, stir together remaining ingredients except garnish. Add egg mixture to flour mixture; stir until blended. Pour batter by ⅓ cupfuls onto a preheated, lightly greased waffle iron. Bake according to manufacturer's instructions. Serve topped with fresh raspberries and maple syrup.

Oatmeal Waffles

Robin Hill, *Rochester, NY*

Warm Country Gingerbread Waffles

Serve with brown sugar, powdered sugar, hot maple syrup or raspberries.

Makes nine 4-inch waffles

2 c. all-purpose flour
1 t. cinnamon
½ t. ground ginger
½ t. salt
1 c. molasses
½ c. butter
1½ t. baking soda
1 c. buttermilk
1 egg, beaten

Combine flour, cinnamon, ginger and salt. Heat molasses and butter in a saucepan until butter melts. Remove from heat and stir in baking soda. Add buttermilk and egg; fold in flour mixture. Cook in a preheated greased waffle iron according to manufacturer's instructions.

Carol Field Dahlstrom, *Ankeny, IA*

Chocolate Waffle Ice Cream Treats

Ice cream between crisp chocolate waffles... what could be better for dessert or even for a sweet treat on a special day? We made our sandwiches in a mini waffle iron, but you can use a standard waffle iron and break into four pieces, using two for each sandwich.

Serves 6

1 c. chocolate milk
1 egg, beaten
2 T. butter, melted
2 T. baking cocoa powder
1 c. buttermilk biscuit baking mix
½ gal. peppermint ice cream, softened
Garnish: sprinkles

Combine milk, egg and butter in a large bowl. Add baking cocoa and baking mix; whisk until smooth. Add ¾ cup batter for regular waffle iron or ⅓ cup for mini waffle iron to a preheated, greased waffle iron. Bake according to manufacturer's directions. To serve, top each waffle with ice cream and top with other waffle for top. Roll in sprinkles. Wrap in plastic wrap and freeze until ready to serve.

Chocolate Waffle Ice Cream Treats

Barbara McCurry, *Carpinteria, CA*

Barbara's Open-House Waffles

Every Saturday morning, I serve these for family & friends...it's fun, and the neighbors love it!

Serves 6 to 8

3 c. biscuit baking mix
1 c. millet flour
$\frac{1}{8}$ t. baking soda
$\frac{1}{4}$ c. canola oil
3 eggs, beaten
3 c. buttermilk
2 T. water
Garnish: maple syrup, fresh strawberries,
   whipped cream

In a bowl, whisk together baking mix, flour and baking soda. Add remaining ingredients except garnish and mix well. Drop batter by $\frac{1}{2}$ cupfuls onto a heated waffle iron; cook according to manufacturer's directions. Top with maple syrup, strawberries and whipped cream.

Nicole Millard, *Mendon, MI*

Grandma McKindley's Waffles

You can't go wrong with an old-fashioned waffle breakfast...the topping choices are endless.

Serves 4

2 c. all-purpose flour
1 T. baking powder
$\frac{1}{4}$ t. salt
2 eggs, separated
$1\frac{1}{2}$ c. milk
3 T. butter, melted
Garnish: butter, syrup

Sift together flour, baking powder and salt in a large bowl; set aside. In another bowl, beat egg whites with an electric mixer at high speed until stiff; set aside. Stir together egg yolks, milk and melted butter in a separate bowl; add to dry ingredients, stirring just until moistened. Fold in egg whites. Ladle batter by $\frac{1}{2}$ cupfuls onto a lightly greased preheated waffle iron; bake according to manufacturer's directions. Serve with additional butter and syrup.

Grandma McKindley's Waffles

Melanie Lowe, *Dover, DE*

Herb Waffles

Serve these flavorful waffles alongside scrambled eggs or topped with a scoop of your favorite creamed chicken.

Makes 4 servings

2 c. all-purpose flour
2 T. sugar
4 t. baking powder
1 t. salt
2 T. fresh chives, snipped
1 T. fresh thyme, snipped
1 T. fresh flat-leaf parsley, snipped
1 T. fresh sage, snipped
1½ c. milk
½ c. plus 2 T. butter
2 eggs, beaten

In a large bowl, mix together flour, sugar, baking powder and salt; stir in herbs. In a saucepan over low heat, warm milk and butter together until butter is melted. Cool slightly; whisk in eggs, then flour mixture. Pour ¾ cup batter per waffle onto a preheated, buttered waffle iron. Bake according to manufacturer's directions, until crisp and golden.

Holly Meurisse, *South Jordan, UT*

Quick English Muffin Sandwiches

We just moved here and I am so busy right now. I love these sandwiches because they are quick to make and everyone loves them.

Makes 6 servings

6 English muffins, split
6 slices Cheddar cheese
6 slices thinly sliced ham
Garnish: Dijon mustard

Preheat waffle iron to medium-high; spray with non-stick vegetable spray. Assemble the sandwiches using the English muffins, cheese and ham. Working in batches, place sandwich in waffle iron. Close gently; cook until crisp and golden about 3 to 4 minutes. Serve immediately with Dijon mustard.

Quick English Muffin Sandwiches

Constance Bockstoce, *Dallas, GA*

Special Waffle Sandwiches

One day I was out of bread for sandwiches. I thought. "Why not use waffles instead?" It's become a family favorite! Some combos we like are egg & sausage sandwiches for breakfast, rotisserie chicken salad sandwiches for lunch and Sloppy Joe sandwiches (swap out the cheese to sharp Cheddar) for a hearty dinner sandwich.

Makes 4 to 6 servings

2 c. biscuit baking mix
1½ c. water
2 T. olive oil
8-oz. pkg. finely shredded Swiss cheese
8 to 12 slices deli baked ham
2 to 3 ripe tomatoes, sliced
mayonnaise or other sandwich spread to taste

In a bowl, combine baking mix, water, oil and cheese; mix well. Add ¾ cup batter per waffle to a greased waffle iron. Bake according to manufacturer's directions. Divide waffles into quarters. Top half of the waffle quarters with ham, tomato and mayonnaise; top with remaining quarters.

Denny Bailey, *Des Moines, IA*

Cornbread & Bacon Waffles

We love cornbread and this is one of our favorite ways to serve it. The waffle iron makes it so crispy and good!

Serves 6

1 c. cornmeal
1 c. all-purpose flour
4 T. sugar
1 t. baking soda
1 t. baking powder
½ t. salt
¼ c. butter, melted
2 eggs, beaten
1½ c. buttermilk
2 T. real bacon bits
½ c. frozen corn
1 t. olive oil
Optional: toasted corn

In a bowl, combine cornmeal, flour, sugar, baking soda, baking powder and salt. Make a well in the middle and add butter, eggs and buttermilk; mix well. Fold in bacon bits and frozen corn. Add ¾ cup batter per waffle to a greased waffle iron. Bake according to manufacturer's directions. To toast corn, add frozen corn to a skillet with olive oil. Cook until golden, about 2 minutes. Garnish waffles with toasted corn sprinkled on top, if desired.

Cornbread & Bacon Waffles

Sheet Pan Recipes

The humble sheet pan has many variations. Some call them baking sheets or half sheets depending on their size. They can be aluminum, non-stick, insulated, black steel or heavy gauge. Unlike cookie sheets which have no rolled edges, sheet pans can be used in a variety of ways. You can roast, bake, broil or grill with them. They are a versatile friend to have in the kitchen. Need a quick breakfast with little clean-up? Try making a Rise & Shine Breakfast Pizza or Yummy Sausage Cups. Appetizers are so easy when you make them on a sheet pan. Whip up a batch of Cheddar-Chive Bites or Prosciutto-Wrapped Asparagus in no time. Santa Fe Grilled Veggie Pizza and Greek Pita Pizza are all-time favorites baked in a hot oven. So look at that sheet pan in a different way...it will make cooking and clean-up so easy for you, leaving you plenty of extra family time.

Mel Chencharick, *Julian, PA*

Veggie Mini Pizzas

Add other toppings to these little pizzas if you like, such as sliced onion or pepper.

Serves 6

6 pita rounds or flatbreads
1½ c. pizza or pasta sauce
1 c. baby spinach
1 c. shredded mozzarella cheese
2 plum tomatoes, sliced

Place pita rounds on an ungreased baking sheet. Spread each with ¼ cup sauce; top with spinach, cheese and tomato. Bake pizzas at 350 degrees for 15 to 20 minutes, or until cheese is bubbly.

Tiffany Brinkley, *Broomfield, CO*

Town Square Favorite

A visit with friends for the weekend took us to a farmers' market on the town square. We filled our baskets with veggies, herbs, even cheese! That same day, we made these yummy open-faced sandwiches for dinner on a simple sheet pan.

Serves 4

3 T. butter
1½ c. sliced mushrooms
½ c. red onion, sliced and separated into rings
2 zucchini, thinly sliced
1 t. dried basil
½ t. garlic, finely chopped
¼ t. salt
¼ t. pepper
4 whole-wheat bagel thins, split
1 c. shredded Monterey Jack cheese, divided
2 tomatoes, sliced

Melt butter in a skillet over medium heat. Stir in all ingredients except bagels, cheese and tomatoes. Cook, stirring occasionally, until vegetables are crisp-tender, about 4 to 5 minutes. Arrange bagels on an ungreased baking sheet. Sprinkle one tablespoon cheese over each bagel half. Bake at 375 degrees for 5 minutes, or until cheese is melted. Remove from oven; top each with one slice tomato. Spoon on vegetable mixture; top with remaining cheese. Continue baking 4 to 5 minutes longer, until cheese is melted. Serve open-faced.

Town Square Favorite

Angie Walsh, *Cedar Rapids, IA*

Yummy Sausage Cups

We enjoy having these on Christmas day, but they're good any time of year. My mother-in-law makes them, and they are a huge hit!

Makes 5 dozen, serves 30

1 lb. maple-flavored ground pork breakfast sausage
8-oz. pkg. shredded sharp Cheddar cheese
16-oz. container sour cream
1-oz. pkg. ranch salad dressing mix
4 2.1-oz. pkgs. frozen phyllo cups

Brown sausage in a skillet over medium heat; drain and return to skillet. Stir in remaining ingredients except phyllo cups. Fill each phyllo cup with a scoop of sausage mixture. Arrange cups on ungreased baking sheets. Bake at 350 degrees for 15 minutes, or until heated through and cups are golden.

Jennifer Hansen, *Escanaba, MI*

Sunrise Granola

Carry this amazing granola with you on an early morning hike. It will give you energy and it tastes super-good as well!

Makes about 2 cups

1 c. long-cooking oats, uncooked
¼ c. unsweetened flaked coconut
2 T. sunflower seeds
¼ c. wheat germ
¼ t. cinnamon
1 T. honey
¼ t. vanilla extract
2 t. canola oil

In a large mixing bowl, combine oats, coconut, sunflower seeds, wheat germ and cinnamon. In a separate bowl, combine honey, vanilla and oil; blend well. Pour honey mixture into oat mixture; blend well. Spread on a baking sheet and bake at 350 degrees for 20 to 25 minutes, stirring every 5 minutes. Let cool, then store in an airtight jar.

Sunrise Granola

Ann Farris, *Biscoe, AR*

Prosciutto-Wrapped Asparagus

This simple and pretty presentation of asparagus is always a hit at any party or event.

Serves 6

1 bunch asparagus, about 10 pieces, trimmed
1 T. olive oil
1 t. kosher salt
1 t. pepper
3-oz. pkg. sliced prosciutto, cut into strips with fat removed
Optional: lemon slices

Toss asparagus with oil, salt and pepper. Arrange in a single layer on an ungreased rimmed baking sheet. Bake at 400 degrees for 5 minutes. Allow to cool slightly. Wrap each asparagus spear with a strip of prosciutto. Return to oven and bake for 4 more minutes or until asparagus is crisp-tender and prosciutto is slightly browned. Serve warm or at room temperature, garnished with thin lemon slices, if desired.

Micki Stephens, *Marion, OH*

Rise & Shine Breakfast Pizza

You will enjoy tasting the layers of all your breakfast favorites in this dish!

Serves 8 to 10

2-lb. pkg. frozen shredded hashbrowns
1½ c. shredded Cheddar cheese, divided
7 eggs, beaten
½ c. milk
salt and pepper to taste
8 to 10 pork breakfast sausage patties, cooked

Prepare hashbrowns according to package directions; spread on an ungreased baking sheet or pizza pan. Top with ½ cup cheese; set aside. Whisk together eggs and milk in a microwave-safe bowl; microwave on high 3 minutes, then scramble eggs well with a whisk. Return to microwave and cook 3 more minutes; whisk well to scramble. Layer eggs on top of cheese; add salt and pepper to taste. Top with remaining cheese. Arrange sausage patties on top. Bake at 400 degrees for 10 minutes, or until cheese is melted. Cut into squares or wedges to serve.

Rise & Shine Breakfast Pizza

Connie Hilty, *Pearland, TX*

Breakfast Pizza

Is there anything better than pizza for breakfast? You are going to love this recipe!

Serves 2 to 4

11-oz. tube refrigerated thin-crust pizza dough
14-oz. can pizza sauce
16-oz. container ricotta cheese
¼ c. fresh oregano, chopped
favorite pizza toppings
4 eggs
salt and pepper to taste

Roll out dough into a 13-inch by 9-inch rectangle; transfer to a greased rimmed baking sheet. Spread pizza sauce on dough, leaving a ½-inch border. Top with cheese, oregano and other pizza toppings. Bake at 500 degrees for 4 to 5 minutes, or until crust begins to turn golden. Crack each egg into a small bowl and slip onto pizza, being careful not to break the yolks. Bake for another 5 minutes, until eggs are done as desired.

Mary Ann Lewis, *Olive Branch, MS*

Best-Ever Breakfast Bars

These chewy, healthy bars are perfect to grab in the morning for a perfect take-along breakfast.

Makes 12 bars, serves 12

1 c. Sunrise Granola (see page 178) or favorite granola
1 c. quick-cooking oats, uncooked
½ c. all-purpose flour
¼ c. brown sugar, packed
⅛ t. cinnamon
½ c. unsalted mixed nuts, coarsely chopped
½ c. dried fruit, chopped into small pieces
2 T. ground flaxseed meal
¼ c. canola oil
⅓ c. honey
½ t. vanilla extract
1 egg, beaten

Combine granola and the next 7 ingredients in a large bowl. Whisk together oil, honey and vanilla; stir into granola mixture. Add egg; stir to blend Press mixture into a parchment paper-lined 9"x7" sheet pan. Bake at 325 degrees for 30 to 35 minutes, until lightly golden around the edges. Remove from oven and cool 30 minutes to one hour. Slice into bars.

Best-Ever Breakfast Bars

Michelle Powell, *Valley, AL*

Mexican Roasted Cauliflower

So quick and tasty...you'll make this recipe often!

Makes 6 servings

3 T. olive oil
3 cloves garlic, minced
1 T. chili powder, or to taste
½ t. dried cumin
1 lb. cauliflower, cut into bite-size flowerets
juice of 1 lime
¼ c. fresh cilantro, chopped

Mix oil, garlic and spices in a large bowl. Add the cauliflower; toss to coat. Spread on an ungreased baking sheet. Bake, uncovered, at 325 degrees for one hour and 15 minutes, stirring occasionally. Remove from oven. Drizzle with lime juice; sprinkle with cilantro and toss well. Serve warm.

Jean Martin, *Hingham, MA*

Cheddar-Chive Bites

These little cheesy gems are always a hit at our card parties. Using biscuit mix makes them so easy. Sometimes I add just a little shaved ham along with the cucumber and radishes... everyone loves those as well.

Makes 2 to 3 dozen

2½ c. biscuit baking mix
1 c. shredded Cheddar cheese
¾ c. milk
⅛ t. garlic powder
6 T. butter, melted and divided
3 T. fresh chives, snipped and divided
2 5-oz. containers garlic & herb cheese spread, softened
Garnish: thinly sliced cucumber and radish

Combine baking mix, cheese, milk, garlic powder and 2 tablespoons butter; mix well. Drop by tablespoonfuls onto ungreased baking sheets. Bake at 400 degrees for 10 to 12 minutes, just until golden. Mix remaining butter and one tablespoon chives; brush over warm biscuits. Split biscuits; set aside. Blend cheese spread and remaining chives. Spread lightly onto bottom halves of biscuits; add cucumber, radish and top halves.

Cheddar-Chive Bites

Jo Ann, *Gooseberry Patch*

Baja Shrimp Quesadillas

These quesadillas are always a special treat with all the yummy ingredients inside each tasty little serving. Everyone loves them!

Makes about 4 dozen

2 ½ lbs. shrimp, peeled and cleaned
3 c. shredded Cheddar cheese
½ c. mayonnaise
¾ c. salsa
¼ t. ground cumin
¼ t. cayenne pepper
¼ t. pepper
12 6-inch flour tortillas
Garnish: plain Greek yogurt, chopped fresh
   parsley

Chop shrimp, discarding tails. Mix shrimp, cheese, mayonnaise, salsa, cumin and peppers; spread one to 2 tablespoons on one tortilla. Place another tortilla on top; put on a greased baking sheet. Repeat with remaining tortillas. Bake at 350 degrees for 15 minutes; remove and cut into small triangles. Garnish as desired.

Rhonda Johnson, *Studio City, CA*

Bruschetta with Cranberry Relish

I love these bruschetta because they taste so good, but also because they are so pretty!

Serves 16

1 large whole-grain baguette loaf, sliced ¼-inch
   thick
1 to 2 T. olive oil
1 t. orange zest
1 t. lemon zest
½ c. chopped pecans
½ c. crumbled low-fat blue cheese

Brush baguette slices lightly with oil. Arrange on a sheet pan; toast lightly under broiler. Turn slices over; spread with Cranberry Relish. Sprinkle with zests, pecans and blue cheese. Place under broiler just until cheese begins to melt.

CRANBERRY RELISH:

16-oz. can whole-berry cranberry sauce
6-oz. pkg. sweetened dried cranberries
½ c. sugar
1 t. rum extract
1 c. chopped pecans

Stir all ingredients together.

Bruschetta with Cranberry Relish

Rachel Rowden, *Festus, MO*

Busy Mom's Biscuit Cheeseburger Pizza

This is a go-to for my family of four on those nights we have softball and tee ball practice. My 12-year-old daughter Isabella and 6-year-old daughter Carly both love this recipe.

Makes 8 servings

1 lb. ground beef
1 T. dried minced onion
salt and pepper to taste
10³/₄-oz. can Cheddar cheese soup
16-oz. tube refrigerated biscuits
1 c. shredded Cheddar cheese
Garnish: cheeseburger condiments

Brown beef in a skillet with onion; drain and season with salt and pepper. Stir in soup; set aside. Stretch biscuits and press together to form a crust; place on a baking sheet sprayed with non-stick vegetable spray. Top crust with beef mixture; sprinkle evenly with cheese. Bake at 350 degrees for 10 minutes or until crust is golden and cheese is melted. Cut into squares; serve with your favorite condiments.

Diane Williams, *Mountain Top, PA*

Simple Stromboli

I like ham in my stromboli, but my husband likes beef in his...so I make both kinds!

Serves 4

1 green pepper, thinly sliced
1 onion, thinly sliced
1 T. butter
13.8-oz. tube refrigerated pizza crust
½ lb. deli baked ham or roast beef, thinly sliced
8 slices mozzarella cheese
pepper to taste

In a skillet over medium heat, sauté green pepper and onion in butter until tender. Unroll unbaked pizza crust on a lightly greased baking sheet. Layer crust with slices of meat and cheese; top with green pepper mixture and season with pepper. Roll crust loosely into a tube, jelly-roll style; pinch top and sides closed. Bake, seam-side down, at 375 degrees for about 25 minutes, until golden. Slice to serve.

Simple Stromboli

Dobbie Hull, *Lubbock, TX*

Buttermilk Cinnamon Rolls

These no-yeast cinnamon rolls disappear fast!

Serves 15

3 c. all-purpose flour
4 t. baking powder
¼ t. baking soda
1 t. salt
½ c. cold butter
1½ c. buttermilk
¼ c. butter, softened
½ c. sugar
1 t. cinnamon

In a large bowl, combine first 4 ingredients; cut in cold butter until crumbs form. Stir in buttermilk until well blended; knead dough on a lightly floured surface for 4 to 5 minutes. Roll out to ¼-inch thickness; spread softened butter over dough to edges. In a small bowl, mix sugar and cinnamon; sprinkle over dough. Roll up jelly-roll style; cut into ½-inch slices. Place on 2 greased baking sheets; bake at 400 degrees for 10 to 12 minutes.

Joyce LaMure, *Sequim, WA*

Cranberry-Orange Scones

I received this recipe from a friend a few years ago. They're not only yummy, but quick & easy to make.

Serves 10

2 c. biscuit baking mix
½ c. sugar
½ c. butter, softened
1 egg, beaten
½ c. dried cranberries
½ c. chopped pecans
1 T. orange zest
3 T. buttermilk
Garnish: beaten egg white, sanding sugar

Combine baking mix, sugar and butter until crumbly. Make a well in the center and add egg; stir to blend. Stir in cranberries, pecans and zest. Add buttermilk as needed for dough to form a soft ball. Place dough on lightly floured surface and knead 3 or 4 times. Flatten dough and shape into an 8-inch circle. Using a serrated knife, cut dough in triangles. Brush with egg white and garnish with sugar. Arrange on a lightly oiled baking sheet and bake at 400 degrees for 10 to 15 minutes, or until golden.

Cranberry-Orange Scones

Lynda McCormick, *Burkburnett, TX*

Greek Pita Pizza

These little pizzas are so easy to make and are so good for you!

Makes 8 servings

10-oz. pkg. frozen chopped spinach, thawed
    and well drained
4 green onions, chopped
1 T. fresh dill, chopped
garlic salt and pepper to taste
4 whole-wheat pita rounds, split
4 roma tomatoes, sliced ½-inch thick
½ c. crumbled feta cheese with basil & tomato
dried oregano or Greek seasoning to taste

Mix spinach, onions and dill in a small bowl. Season with garlic salt and pepper; set aside. Place pita rounds on ungreased baking sheets. Arrange tomato slices among pitas. Spread spinach mixture evenly over tomatoes; spread cheese over tomatoes. Sprinkle with desired seasoning. Bake at 450 degrees for 10 to 15 minutes, until crisp. Cut into wedges.

April Jacobs, *Loveland, CO*

Santa Fe Grilled Veggie Pizza

Make sure to cut the vegetables into equal-size pieces so that they will grill evenly.

Serves 4

1 to 2 T. all-purpose flour
10-oz. tube refrigerated pizza crust dough
1 lb. portabella mushrooms, stems removed
1 red pepper, quartered
1 yellow pepper, quartered
1 zucchini, cut lengthwise into ½-inch
    thick slices
1 yellow squash, cut lengthwise into ½-inch
    thick slices
¾ t. salt
1 c. Alfredo pasta sauce
1¼ c. smoked mozzarella cheese, shredded

Lightly dust 2 baking sheets with flour. On a lightly floured surface, press dough into a 15-inch by 11-inch rectangle. Cut into quarters; place 2 on each baking sheet. Lightly coat vegetables with non-stick vegetable spray; sprinkle with salt. Grill vegetables over medium-high heat about 10 minutes, or until tender. Cut mushrooms and peppers into slices. Cut zucchini and squash in half crosswise. Grill 2 pieces pizza dough at a time over medium heat for one minute, or until golden. With tongs, turn dough over and grill about 30 more seconds, or until firm. Return to baking sheets. Spread sauce over crusts; top with vegetables and cheese. Grill pizzas, covered, 2 to 3 more minutes, until cheese melts.

Santa Fe Grilled Veggie Pizza

Francie Stutzman, *Dalton, OH*

Italian Bread

We love this bread with homemade vegetable soup or spaghetti...it disappears very quickly!

Makes 3 large loaves

2½ c. water
2 envs. active dry yeast
2 t. salt
¼ c. sugar
¼ c. olive oil
7 c. all-purpose flour
¼ c. cornmeal
1 egg white
1 T. cold water

Heat 2½ cups water until very warm, about 110 to 115 degrees. Dissolve yeast in very warm water in a large bowl. Add salt, sugar and oil; stir well. Stir in flour; mix well. Shape dough into a ball and place in a well-greased bowl, turning to coat top. Cover and let rise one hour, or until double in bulk; punch dough down. Divide dough into 3 equal parts and shape into loaves. Place loaves crosswise on a greased baking sheet that has been sprinkled with cornmeal. Cover and let rise 30 minutes. Cut 4 diagonal slices in the top of each loaf. Bake at 400 degrees for 25 to 30 minutes, until golden. Combine egg white and cold water in a small bowl; whisk well and brush over loaves. Bake 5 more minutes.

Cris Goode, *Mooresville, IN*

Good & Healthy "Fried" Chicken

We love this healthier version of everyone's favorite food...fried chicken!

Makes 5 servings

1 c. whole-grain panko bread crumbs
1 c. cornmeal
2 T. all-purpose flour
salt and pepper to taste
10 chicken drumsticks
1 c. buttermilk

Combine panko, cornmeal, flour, salt and pepper in a gallon-size plastic zipping bag. Coat chicken with buttermilk, one piece at a time. Drop chicken into bag and shake to coat pieces lightly. Arrange chicken on a baking sheet coated with non-stick vegetable spray. Bake, uncovered, at 350 degrees for 40 to 50 minutes, until chicken juices run clear.

> ~ **Kitchen Tip** ~
>
> Keep freshly baked bread warm & toasty... simply slip a piece of aluminum foil into the bread basket, then top it with a decorative napkin or tea towel.

Good & Healthy "Fried" Chicken

Angela Murphy, *Tempe, AZ*

Blue Cheese Cut-Out Crackers

Dress up any salad when you serve these rich blue cheese crackers. Make them in any shape you like or cut them into little squares and skip the cookie cutters!

Makes about 2 dozen

1 c. all-purpose flour
7 T. butter, softened
7 T. crumbled blue cheese
½ t. dried parsley
1 egg yolk
4 t. whipping cream
salt and cayenne pepper to taste

In a medium bowl, mix all ingredients together; let rest for 30 minutes. Roll dough out to about ⅛-inch thick. Use small cookie cutters to cut out crackers. Bake on ungreased baking sheets at 400 degrees for 8 to 10 minutes, just until golden. Let cool; remove carefully. Store in an airtight container.

Andrea Durante, *Hopedale, MA*

Southwestern Smothered Potato Chips

The chips are yummy all by themselves, but when you add the onion and cheese they become a much-talked-about appetizer or side dish. We love them with the guacamole and salsa too!

Serves 4 to 6

6 potatoes, sliced lengthwise ⅛-inch thick
½ t. salt
2 T. olive oil
½ c. red onion, chopped
1 c. shredded Monterey Jack cheese
1 c. guacamole
1 c. salsa

Arrange potato slices in a single layer on a lightly greased baking sheet. Sprinkle with salt; drizzle with oil. Broil under low heat for about 10 minutes, until crisp but not burnt, checking often. Remove from oven. Sprinkle chips evenly with onion and cheese. Bake at 350 degrees for 5 minutes, until cheese is melted. To serve, top with small dollops of guacamole and salsa.

Southwesten Smothered Potato Chips

Jewel Grindey, *Lindenhurst, IL*

Seeded Tortilla Crisps

Serve these with your favorite dipping sauce for a fun and easy appetizer or snack.

Makes about 2½ dozen, serves 12

2 T. butter, melted
8 10-inch flour tortillas
½ c. grated Parmesan cheese
1 egg white, beaten
Garnish: sesame, poppy and/or caraway seed,
    onion powder, cayenne pepper or dried cumin

Brush butter lightly over one side of each tortilla; sprinkle evenly with cheese and press down lightly. Carefully turn tortillas over. Brush other side with egg white and sprinkle with desired seeds and seasoning. Cut each tortilla into 4 strips with a pastry cutter or knife. Place strips cheese-side down on a baking sheet sprayed with non-stick vegetable spray. Bake at 400 degrees, on middle rack of oven, for about 8 to 10 minutes, until crisp and golden. Cool on a wire rack.

Linda Diepholz, *Lakeville, MN*

Baked Chicken Chimichangas

I have been making these chicken chimis for years. I like that they are baked and not deep-fried...much healthier. People who don't even like Mexican food discover they love these. I make this recipe often and I even like the leftovers cold!

Serves 4 to 6

2 c. cooked chicken, chopped
    or shredded
1 c. salsa or picante sauce
2 c. shredded Cheddar cheese
4 green onions, chopped
1½ t. ground cumin
1 t. dried oregano
8 8-inch flour tortillas
2 T. butter, melted
Garnish: additional shredded cheese, green
    onions, salsa

In a bowl, combine chicken, salsa or sauce, cheese, onions and seasonings. Spoon ⅓ cup of mixture down the center of each tortilla; fold opposite sides over filling. Roll up from bottom and place seam-side down on an ungreased baking sheet. Brush with melted butter. Bake, uncovered, at 400 degrees for 30 minutes or until golden, turning halfway through cooking. Garnish with additional cheese and onions; serve with salsa on the side, as desired.

Baked Chicken Chimichangas

Melissa Fraser, *Valencia, CA*

Cinnamon Crisps

These little crispy treats are fun to make with the kids. Make plenty because they will go fast!

Makes about 2½ dozen, serves 8

½ t. vanilla extract
1 T. hot water
½ t. cinnamon
3 T. sugar
4 6-inch flour tortillas, each cut into 8 wedges

Combine vanilla and water in a cup; blend cinnamon and sugar in a separate cup. Brush vanilla mixture over both sides of tortilla wedges; sprinkle with cinnamon-sugar. Place on a baking sheet sprayed with non-stick vegetable spray. Bake at 450 degrees for 5 minutes, until crisp.

> ⚬ **Making it Special** ⚬
>
> Serve these cinnamon crisps in little paper cups that the kids can carry around and snack on as they play.

Rita Morgan, *Pueblo, CO*

Herbed Cheese Focaccia

This savory bread is a favorite, scrumptious for snacking or to accompany a tossed salad.

Serves 12 to 14

13.8-oz. tube refrigerated pizza dough
1 onion, finely chopped
2 cloves garlic, minced
2 T. olive oil
1 t. dried basil
1 t. dried oregano
½ t. dried rosemary
1 c. shredded mozzarella cheese

Unroll dough on a greased baking sheet. Press with fingers to form indentations; set aside. Sauté onion and garlic in oil in a skillet; remove from heat. Stir in herbs; spread mixture evenly over dough. Sprinkle with cheese. Bake at 400 degrees for 10 to 15 minutes, until golden.

Herbed Cheese Focaccia

Suzanne Morley, Kent, England

Salmon Loaf Dip

This appetizer is always the hit of the party. You can mix up the ingredients ahead of time and keep in the fridge until you are ready to fill the bread bowl and bake right before the party.

Serves 4 to 8

1 large loaf crusty bread
1 onion, finely chopped
1 to 2 t. oil
8-oz. pkg. cream cheese, softened
2 7¾-oz. cans salmon, drained
3 to 4 T. sour cream
1 t. hot pepper sauce
⅛ t. salt
⅛ t. pepper
1 t. fresh dill weed, chopped

Slice the top from bread loaf. Hollow out center and cut bread into cubes, if desired; set aside. Sauté onion in oil in a medium saucepan over medium heat until tender. Place onion and remaining ingredients in a medium bowl; mix well. Spoon mixture into hollow loaf; replace bread lid and place on an ungreased baking sheet. Bake at 350 degrees for 30 minutes. Add reserved bread cubes to baking sheet, bake both for 3 to 5 more minutes. Serve dip with warmed bread cubes.

Barb Bargdill, Gooseberry Patch

Cheesy Tuna Triangles

It's the sweet raisin bread and chopped apple that make these sandwiches stand out from all the rest.

Makes 12 servings

1 T. oil
1 c. apple, cored and chopped
3 T. onion, chopped
7-oz. can albacore tuna, drained
¼ c. chopped walnuts
¼ c. mayonnaise
2 t. lemon juice
⅛ t. salt
⅛ t. pepper
6 slices raisin bread, toasted and halved
    diagonally
6 slices sharp Cheddar cheese, halved diagonally

Heat oil in a skillet over medium heat; add apple and onion. Cook, stirring occasionally, about 5 minutes until tender. Remove from heat; transfer to a bowl. Stir in tuna, walnuts, mayonnaise, lemon juice, salt and pepper. Place toast slices on an ungreased baking sheet. Top with tuna mixture and a slice of cheese. Broil 4 to 5 inches from heat for 3 to 4 minutes, or until cheese begins to melt.

Cheesy Tuna Triangles

Dale Duncan, *Waterloo, IA*

Bacon & Egg Potato Skins

A tummy-filling complete meal in a potato skin...yummy!

Makes 4 servings

2 baking potatoes
4 eggs, beaten
1 to 2 t. butter
salt and pepper to taste
¼ c. shredded Monterey Jack cheese
¼ c. shredded Cheddar cheese
4 slices bacon, crisply cooked and crumbled
Garnish: sour cream, chopped fresh chives

Bake potatoes at 400 degrees for one hour, until tender. Slice potatoes in half lengthwise; scoop out centers and reserve for another recipe. Place potato skins on a lightly greased baking sheet. Bake at 400 degrees for 6 to 8 minutes, until crisp. In a skillet over medium heat, scramble eggs in butter just until they begin to set. Add salt and pepper; remove from heat. Spoon equal amounts of eggs, cheeses and bacon into each potato skin. Reduce heat to 350 degrees and bake for 7 to 10 minutes, until cheese is melted and eggs are completely set. Garnish with sour cream and chives.

Jessica Kraus, *Delaware, OH*

Jalapeño Popper Pinwheels

This is such a great recipe for football season. Using the can of crescent rolls makes it super easy so you don't have to miss any of the game!

Makes 8

4-oz. can diced jalapeño peppers, drained
8-oz. pkg. cream cheese, softened
1 c. shredded Mexican-blend cheese
2 t. salt
8-oz. tube refrigerated crescent rolls
grated Parmesan cheese to taste

In a large bowl, combine jalapeños, cheeses and salt; blend well and set aside. Unroll crescent rolls; seal seams but do not separate. Spread cream cheese mixture evenly over the dough. Roll up jelly-roll style; slice the roll into ⅓-inch slices. Arrange on a lightly greased baking sheet, leaving one inch between slices. Dust with Parmesan cheese. Bake at 375 degrees for 11 to 15 minutes, until tops begin to turn golden. Let cool for a minute, then transfer to a cooling rack.

Jalapeño Popper Pinwheels

Leslie Williams, *Americus, GA*

Maple-Pecan Brunch Ring

A sweet & simple way to make a tasty treat for guests.

Makes about 12 servings

¾ c. chopped pecans
½ c. brown sugar, packed
2 t. cinnamon
2 17.3-oz. tubes refrigerated jumbo flaky biscuits
2 T. butter, melted
½ c. maple syrup

Combine pecans, brown sugar and cinnamon; set aside. Split each biscuit horizontally; brush half of the biscuits with butter and sprinkle with half the pecan mixture. Arrange topped biscuits in a circle on an ungreased baking sheet; overlap each biscuit slightly and keep within 2 inches of the edge of the baking sheet. Brush remaining biscuit halves with butter; sprinkle with remaining pecan mixture. Arrange a second ring just inside the first ring, overlapping edges. Bake at 350 degrees for 30 to 35 minutes, until golden. Remove to wire rack; cool 10 minutes. Brush with maple syrup.

Rita Morgan, *Pueblo, CO*

Southwestern Flatbread

Yum...hot fresh-baked bread to enjoy for breakfast with a cup of fresh fruit! Easy to change up to Italian flavors too, with oregano and Parmesan cheese.

Makes about 15 pieces

2 t. olive oil, divided
11-oz. tube refrigerated crusty French loaf
½ c. roasted sunflower kernels
1 t. chili powder
½ to 1 t. coarse salt

Brush a 15"x10" sheet pan with one teaspoon oil; unroll dough onto pan. Use a floured rolling pin to roll out into a rectangle. Drizzle dough with remaining oil; brush over dough. In a small bowl, combine sunflower kernels and chili powder; mix well and sprinkle over the dough. Firmly press sunflower kernels into dough; sprinkle top with salt. Bake at 375 degrees for 12 to 16 minutes, until golden. Remove flatbread to a wire rack; cool 10 minutes. Tear or cut into pieces.

Southwestern Flatbread

Skillet Recipes

Good cooks love their favorite skillet and now we know why. You can take this sturdy, no-nonsense item from stovetop to oven. You can sauté in it, bake in it and fry in it. This kitchen essential has been around for years and continues to showcase your favorite foods with little effort. Start your day with a Festive Brunch Frittata served right from the cast-iron skillet. They will flip over personalized omelets like an Asparagus & Mushroom Omelet or a Hashbrown Skillet Omelet. Want a simple one-skillet dinner? Our Skillet Goulash or Dad's Cajun Dinner are meals you can make in no time with only one pan to clean. Nothing works better for fried foods than a cast-iron skillet. Dixie Fried Chicken and Chicken-Fried Steak are two favorites. So plan your next meal with your skillet in mind, letting this kitchen friend do the heavy lifting for you while you enjoy time to spare.

Wendy Paffenroth, *Pine Island, NY*

Apple-Stuffed French Toast

Treat your family to this delectable French toast, filled with brown sugar-sweetened apples.

Makes 4 servings

3 apples, peeled, cored and cut into chunks
¼ c. brown sugar, packed
cinnamon to taste
2 eggs, beaten
½ c. milk
1 t. vanilla extract
8 slices wheat bread
Garnish: maple syrup

In a saucepan, combine apples, brown sugar, cinnamon and a small amount of water. Cover and simmer over medium-low heat for 5 to 10 minutes, until apples are soft; set aside. Heat a greased cast-iron skillet over medium heat. In a bowl, whisk together eggs, milk and vanilla. Quickly dip bread into egg mixture, coating both sides; place in skillet. Cook until golden on both sides. To serve, place one slice of French toast on a plate; top with a scoop of apple mixture and another slice of French toast. Drizzle with maple syrup.

Renae Scheiderer, *Beallsville, OH*

Festive Brunch Frittata

Serve this delicious egg dish in the skillet that you cook it in for a fun and rustic look...and clean-up is quick!

Serves 6

8 eggs, beaten
½ t. salt
⅛ t. pepper
½ c. shredded Cheddar cheese
2 T. butter
2 c. red, green and yellow peppers, chopped
¼ c. onion, chopped
Garnish: chopped fresh parsley

Beat together eggs, salt and pepper. Fold in cheese and set aside. Melt butter over medium heat in a 10" non-stick, oven-safe skillet. Add peppers and onion to skillet; sauté until tender. Pour eggs over peppers and onion; don't stir. Cover and cook over medium-low heat for about 9 minutes. Eggs are set when frittata is lightly golden on the underside. Turn oven on broil. Move skillet from stovetop to oven; broil top about 5 inches from heat until lightly golden. Garnish with parsley.

Festive Brunch Frittata

Vickie, *Gooseberry Patch*

Farmhouse Sausage Patties

Spice 'em just the way your family likes! Serve alongside scrambled eggs and hashbrowns.

Serves 6

1 lb. ground pork
1 t. ground cumin
½ t. dried thyme
½ t. dried sage
1 t. salt
½ t. pepper
Optional: ⅛ t. cayenne pepper

Combine all ingredients; mix well. Cover and refrigerate overnight to allow flavors to blend. Form into 6 patties. Arrange in a lightly greased cast-iron skillet and brown both sides over medium heat until no pink remains.

Audrey Lett, *Newark, DE*

Asparagus & Mushroom Omelet

A delicious way to savor the first tender asparagus of springtime. Add a sprinkle of shredded cheese, if you like.

Makes 3 servings

½ lb. asparagus, trimmed and cut into 1-inch pieces
2 T. butter, divided
½ lb. sliced mushrooms
1 clove garlic, minced
4 eggs, lightly beaten
2 T. skim milk
¾ t. dried basil or thyme
½ t. salt
⅛ t. pepper

In a saucepan over medium heat, cover asparagus with water. Bring to a boil and cook until crisp-tender, about 4 minutes; drain. In a skillet over medium heat, melt one tablespoon butter. Sauté mushrooms and garlic in butter until tender and moisture has evaporated, 5 to 7 minutes. Add mushroom mixture to asparagus; keep warm. In a bowl, whisk together eggs, milk and seasonings. Melt remaining butter in skillet; swirl to coat bottom and sides. Add egg mixture. As eggs cook, gently lift up edges with a spatula and let uncooked egg run underneath until set. Spoon asparagus mixture onto one half of omelet. Slide omelet onto a plate; fold over. Cut into wedges.

Asparagus & Mushroom Omelet

Paula Zsiray, *Logan, UT*

Hashbrown Skillet Omelet

Set out the catsup and hot pepper sauce... everyone can spice up their portion as they like.

Serves 6

½ lb. bacon
2 T. oil
3 c. frozen shredded hashbrowns
1½ c. shredded Cheddar or Cheddar Jack cheese, divided
6 eggs, beaten
¼ c. water
1 T. fresh parsley, chopped
½ t. paprika

Cook bacon in a cast-iron skillet over medium-high heat until crisp. Remove bacon to paper towels. Drain skillet; add oil to skillet. Add frozen hashbrowns and cook without turning for about 10 minutes, until golden. Turn carefully; cook other side until golden. Remove skillet from heat. Sprinkle hashbrowns with crumbled bacon and one cup shredded cheese. Beat eggs and water; pour over cheese. Sprinkle with parsley and paprika. Transfer skillet to oven. Bake, uncovered, at 350 degrees for about 20 to 25 minutes, until eggs are set in the center. Remove from oven; sprinkle with remaining cheese and let stand for 5 minutes. Cut into wedges.

Joshua Logan, *Corpus Christi, TX*

Egg & Bacon Quesadillas

I make these quesadillas on weekends when I have plenty of time to enjoy them. Serve with a cup of yogurt or some fresh fruit.

Serves 4

2 T. butter, divided
4 8-inch flour tortillas
5 eggs, beaten
½ c. milk
8-oz. pkg. shredded Cheddar cheese
2 slices bacon, crisply cooked and crumbled
Optional: salsa, sour cream

Lightly spread about ¼ teaspoon butter on one side of each tortilla; set aside. In a bowl, beat eggs and milk until combined. Pour egg mixture into a hot, lightly greased skillet; cook and stir over medium heat until done. Remove scrambled eggs to a dish and keep warm. Melt remaining butter in the skillet and add a tortilla, buttered-side down. Layer with ¼ of the cheese, ½ of the eggs and ½ of the bacon. Top with ¼ of the cheese and a tortilla, buttered-side up. Cook about one to 2 minutes on each side, until golden. Repeat with remaining ingredients. Cut each into 4 wedges and serve with salsa and sour cream, if desired.

Egg & Bacon Quesadillas

Virginia Watson, *Scranton, PA*

Grandma's Warm Breakfast Fruit

Keep this delectable fruit compote warm for brunch in a mini slow cooker.

Serves 6 to 8

3 apples, peeled, cored and thickly sliced
1 orange, peeled and sectioned
¾ c. raisins
½ c. dried plums, chopped
3 c. plus 3 T. water, divided
½ c. sugar
½ t. cinnamon
2 T. cornstarch
Garnish: favorite granola

Combine fruit and 3 cups water in a cast-iron skillet over medium heat. Bring to a boil; reduce heat and simmer for 10 minutes. Stir in sugar and cinnamon. In a small bowl, mix together cornstarch and remaining water; stir into fruit mixture. Bring to a boil, stirring constantly; cook and stir for 2 minutes. Spoon into bowls; top with granola to serve.

Jennifer Gutermuth, *Oshkosh, WI*

Veggie, Egg & Rice Breakfast Bowls

I love eating veggies for breakfast! I use whatever is in my kitchen...red pepper, zucchini, green beans. They are all good in this bowl.

Makes 4 servings

1 T. olive oil
1 lb. asparagus, cut into bite-sized pieces
3 c. fresh spinach leaves
3 c. cabbage, shredded
1½ c. cooked brown rice, warmed
½ c. hummus
1 avocado, peeled, pitted and diced
4 eggs
Garnish: chopped pecans, pumpkin seeds

Heat oil in a skillet over medium-high heat. Add asparagus and sauté for 4 to 5 minutes, stirring occasionally, until tender; set side. In a separate bowl, combine spinach and Honey-Mustard Dressing. Add asparagus, cabbage and rice; toss until combined. Divide spinach mixture evenly among 4 bowls. Top each with hummus and avocado; set aside. To poach eggs, fill a skillet with water and bring to a simmer over medium-high heat. Swirl water with a spoon and gently slide in each egg from a saucer. Cook until set, about 2 minutes. Use a slotted spoon to remove each egg to a bowl. Garnish as desired.

HONEY-MUSTARD DRESSING:

2 T. olive oil
2 T. lemon juice
2 t. mustard
2 T. honey
1 clove garlic, minced
salt and pepper to taste

In a small bowl, whisk together all ingredients.

Veggie, Egg & Rice Breakfast Bowls

Kari Hodges, *Jacksonville, TX*

Skillet Goulash

I like to serve up this old-fashioned family favorite with thick slices of freshly baked sweet cornbread, topped with pats of butter.

Makes 8 to 10 servings

2 lbs. ground beef
10-oz. can diced tomatoes with green chiles
1 lb. redskin potatoes, cut into quarters
15-oz. can tomato sauce
15¼-oz. can corn, drained
14½-oz. can ranch-style beans
salt and pepper to taste
Garnish: shredded Cheddar cheese

Brown beef in a large, deep skillet over medium heat; drain. Add tomatoes with juice and remaining ingredients except garnish; reduce heat. Cover and simmer until potatoes are tender and mixture has thickened, about 45 minutes. Garnish with Cheddar cheese.

Evelyn Bennett, *Salt Lake City, UT*

Easy Eggs Benedict

We love to serve this elegant breakfast when we have company...everyone is always so impressed!

Serves 8

8 eggs
¾ c. light mayonnaise
¼ t. salt
¼ c. whipping cream, whipped
1 t. lemon zest
1 T. lemon juice
4 slices Canadian bacon, halved
4 English muffins, split and toasted

Lightly grease a large skillet; add water to a depth of 2 inches. Bring to a boil; reduce heat, maintaining a light simmer. Working in batches to poach 4 eggs at a time, break eggs, one at a time, into a cup; slip egg into water, holding cup close to water. Simmer 5 minutes or until done. Remove eggs with a slotted spoon; trim edges of eggs, if desired. Set aside. Combine mayonnaise and salt in a small saucepan. Cook over low heat, stirring constantly, 3 minutes. Stir in whipped cream, lemon zest and lemon juice; remove from heat and keep warm. Arrange bacon on muffin halves; top each bacon piece with a poached egg. Spoon reserved sauce over eggs.

Easy Eggs Benedict

Rachel Anderson, *Livermore, CA*

Granny's Country Cornbread

I love to serve this cornbread with tomato jam that I make in the summer.

Makes 8 servings

1¼ c. cornmeal
¾ c. all-purpose flour
5 T. sugar
2 t. baking powder
½ t. salt
1 c. buttermilk
⅓ c. oil
1 egg, beaten
1 c. shredded sharp Cheddar cheese
1 c. canned corn, drained
1 T. jalapeño pepper, minced

Mix together cornmeal, flour, sugar, baking powder and salt in a large bowl. Make a well in center; pour in buttermilk, oil and egg. Stir mixture just until ingredients are lightly moistened. Fold in cheese, corn and jalapeño; pour into a greased 8" cast-iron skillet. Bake at 375 degrees for 20 minutes, or until a tester inserted in the center comes out clean. Let cool slightly; cut into 8 wedges.

Jo Ann, *Gooseberry Patch*

Jo Ann's Garden Frittata

Family & friends are sure to love this savory egg dish. It's filled with brightly colored vegetables...beautiful to look at and delicious to eat.

Makes 8 servings

4 thick slices bacon, chopped
1 onion, diced
1 red pepper, thinly sliced
1 c. corn
1 c. green beans, thinly sliced
1 bunch Swiss chard, thinly sliced
3 eggs, beaten
1¼ c. half-and-half
⅛ t. dried thyme
salt and pepper to taste
1 c. shredded Cheddar cheese

In a large oven-proof skillet over medium- high heat, cook bacon until crisp. Drain bacon on paper towels; reserve drippings. In one tablespoon drippings, sauté onion, red pepper and corn for 5 minutes. Add beans; sauté another 3 minutes. Transfer vegetable mixture to a bowl; set aside. Add one teaspoon drippings to skillet; sauté chard for 2 minutes. Add to vegetable mixture in bowl. In a separate large bowl, whisk eggs, half-and-half and seasonings. Stir in bacon, cheese and vegetable mixture; pour into skillet. Bake at 375 degrees for about 35 minutes, until set and crust is golden. Let stand for 10 minutes; cut into squares.

Jo Ann's Garden Frittata

Sonya Labbe, *Quebec, Canada*

Hashbrown Quiche

A hearty quiche baked in a crust of hashbrowns! Enjoy it for breakfast, or add a zesty salad and have breakfast for dinner.

Serves 4 to 6

3 c. frozen shredded hashbrowns, thawed
1/4 c. butter, melted
3 eggs, beaten
1 c. half-and-half
3/4 c. cooked ham, diced
1/2 c. green onions, chopped
1 c. shredded Cheddar cheese
salt and pepper to taste

In a cast-iron skillet, combine hashbrowns and butter. Press into the bottom and up the sides of skillet. Transfer the skillet to oven. Bake, uncovered, at 450 degrees for 20 to 25 minutes, until crisp and golden. Remove from oven; cool slightly. Combine remaining ingredients in a bowl; pour mixture over the hashbrowns. Reduce the oven temperature to 350 degrees. Bake for another 30 minutes, or until quiche is golden and set.

Linda Bonwill, *Englewood, FL*

Spinach & Tomato French Toast

A healthier way to make French toast...plus, it looks so pretty!

Serves 4

3 eggs
salt and pepper to taste
8 slices Italian bread
4 c. fresh spinach, torn
2 tomatoes, sliced
shaved Parmesan cheese

In a bowl, beat eggs with salt and pepper. Dip bread slices into egg. Place in a lightly greased skillet over medium heat; cook one side until lightly golden. Place fresh spinach, tomato slice and cheese onto each slice, pressing lightly to secure. Flip and briefly cook on other side until cooked. Flip over and serve open-face.

Spinach & Tomato French Toast

Kristen Blanton, *Big Bear City, CA*

Dad's Cajun Dinner

Add more Cajun seasoning and hot pepper sauce if you dare!

Makes 6 servings

1 onion, diced
1 t. garlic, minced
2 T. butter
2 green peppers, diced
5 stalks celery, diced
3 T. Cajun seasoning
14-oz. pkg. Kielbasa, sliced
15-oz. can kidney beans, drained and rinsed
14½-oz. can diced tomatoes
12-oz. can tomato juice
hot pepper sauce to taste
3 c. cooked rice

In a skillet, sauté onion and garlic in butter until onion is crisp-tender. Add peppers, celery and seasoning; continue to sauté until vegetables are tender. Add Kielbasa; sauté an additional 3 to 4 minutes. Add beans, tomatoes and tomato juice; cook until heated through. Sprinkle with hot sauce to taste. Serve over cooked rice.

Evelyn Moriarty, *Philadelphia, PA*

Vegetable Quinoa Patties

This recipe is a family favorite, especially in summertime when fresh-picked veggies are available.

Makes 6 servings

3 eggs
½ c. shredded mozzarella cheese
½ c. cottage cheese
¼ c. whole-wheat flour
1 carrot, peeled and grated
1 zucchini, grated
3 T. green, red or yellow pepper, grated
3 green onions, finely chopped
½ t. ground cumin
¼ t. garlic powder
⅛ t. salt
¼ t. pepper
2 c. cooked quinoa
1 T. olive oil

Beat eggs in a large bowl; stir in cheeses and flour, blending well. Mix in vegetables. Combine seasonings; sprinkle over vegetable mixture and mix well. Add cooked quinoa; stir together well. Heat olive oil in a skillet over medium heat. With a small ladle, drop mixture into skillet, making 6 patties. Flatten lightly with ladle to about ¼-inch thick. Fry patties for 4 to 5 minutes per side, until golden. Serve each serving with 3 tablespoons Dilled Yogurt Dressing.

DILLED YOGURT DRESSING:

½ c. plain Greek yogurt
1 cucumber, peeled and diced
3 sprigs fresh dill, snipped, or ½ t. dill weed

Stir together all ingredients in a small bowl.

Vegetable Quinoa Patties

Jo Ann, *Gooseberry Patch*

Easy Fancy Broccoli

Bagged broccoli flowerets make this side dish a cinch to prepare!

Serves 6

1/3 c. pine nuts
1/4 c. butter
1 T. olive oil
6 cloves garlic, thinly sliced
1 lb. broccoli flowerets
1/2 t. salt
1/8 t. red pepper flakes

Toast pine nuts in a large skillet over medium heat for 6 minutes or until lightly browned. Remove from skillet and set aside. Heat butter and oil in same skillet over medium heat until butter melts. Add garlic; sauté one to 2 minutes or until lightly browned. Add broccoli, salt and red pepper flakes. Sauté for 8 minutes or until broccoli is tender. Stir in pine nuts before serving.

Brenda Rogers, *Atwood, CA*

South-of-the-Border Squash Skillet

Our family grows lots of yellow summer squash in our community garden. We love tacos, so this taco-flavored recipe is a yummy way to use it up! If you omit the meat, it's also a great vegetarian dish.

Makes 4 servings

1 lb. ground beef or turkey
1/3 c. onion, diced
1 c. water
1 1/4-oz. pkg. taco seasoning mix
4 to 5 yellow squash, zucchini or crookneck squash, chopped
1 c. shredded Cheddar cheese

In a skillet over medium heat, brown meat with onion; drain. Stir in water and taco seasoning; add squash. Cover and simmer for about 10 minutes, until squash is tender. Stir in cheese; cover and let stand just until cheese melts.

⟶ Change it Up ⟵

For a change of pace and a little extra spice, use seasoned ground pork sausage instead of beef or turkey in this skillet recipe. You'll love it!

South-of-the-Border Squash Skillet

Wendy Wall, *Battle Creek, MI*

Pepper Jack-Crab Bisque

So easy to make, yet simply splendid! Garnish with a drizzle of cream.

Makes 6 servings

2 T. butter
2 stalks celery, finely chopped
1 onion, finely chopped
2 10¾-oz. cans tomato bisque or tomato soup
2½ c. whipping cream or half-and-half
3 8-oz. pkgs. imitation crabmeat, flaked
1½ c. finely shredded Pepper Jack cheese

Melt butter in a deep cast-iron skillet over medium heat. Add celery and onion; cook until softened. Add bisque or soup, cream or half-and-half and crabmeat. Simmer over low heat until heated through. Stir in cheese until melted. For a thinner consistency, stir in a little more cream or half-and-half as desired.

Sandra Sullivan, *Aurora, CO*

Beef & Snap Pea Stir-Fry

In a rush? Spice up tonight's dinner with my go-to recipe for healthy in a hurry! Substitute chicken or pork for the beef, if you like.

Makes 4 servings

1 c. brown rice, uncooked
1 lb. beef sirloin steak, thinly sliced
1 T. cornstarch
¼ t. salt
¼ t. pepper
2 t. canola oil
¾ c. water
1 lb. sugar snap peas, trimmed and halved
1 red pepper, cut into bite-size pieces
6 green onions, thinly sliced diagonally, white and green parts divided
1 T. fresh ginger, peeled and grated
½ t. red pepper flakes
salt and pepper to taste
2 T. lime juice

Cook rice according to package directions. Fluff with a fork; cover and set aside. Meanwhile, sprinkle beef with cornstarch, salt and pepper; toss to coat. Heat oil in a skillet over medium-high heat. Add half of beef and brown on both sides. Transfer to a plate; repeat with remaining beef. Stir in water, peas, red pepper, white part of onions, ginger and red pepper flakes; season with salt and pepper. Cook until peas turn bright green, one to 2 minutes. Return beef to skillet; cook for another 2 to 3 minutes. Remove from heat. Stir in lime juice and green part of onions. Serve over rice.

Beef & Snap Pea Stir-Fry

Melody Taynor, *Everett, WA*

Lemony Pork Piccata

Serve over quick-cooking angel hair pasta to enjoy every drop of the lemony sauce.

Serves 4

1-lb. pork tenderloin, sliced into 8 portions
2 t. lemon-pepper seasoning
3 T. all-purpose flour
2 T. butter, divided
¼ c. dry sherry or chicken broth
¼ c. lemon juice
¼ c. capers
4 to 6 thin slices lemon

Pound pork slices to ⅛-inch thickness, using a meat mallet or rolling pin. Lightly sprinkle pork with lemon-pepper seasoning and flour. Melt one tablespoon butter in a large skillet over medium-high heat. Add half of prepared pork pieces and sauté 2 to 3 minutes on each side or until golden, turning once. Repeat procedure with remaining butter and pork. Remove pork to a serving plate; set aside. Add sherry or chicken broth, lemon juice, capers and lemon slices to skillet. Cook 2 minutes or until slightly thickened, scraping up browned bits. Add pork and heat thoroughly.

Donna Deeds, *Marysville, TN*

Chicken-Fried Steak

Authentic chicken-fried steak is crunchy outside, tender inside and served with plenty of cream gravy!

Serves 6

2¼ t. salt, divided
1¾ t. pepper, divided
6 4-oz. beef cube steaks
1 sleeve saltine crackers, crushed
1¼ c. all-purpose flour, divided
½ t. baking powder
½ t. cayenne pepper
4¾ c. milk, divided
2 eggs
3½ c. peanut oil
mashed potatoes

Sprinkle ¼ teaspoon each salt and pepper over steaks. Set aside. Combine cracker crumbs, one cup flour, baking powder, one teaspoon salt, ½ teaspoon pepper and cayenne pepper. Whisk together ¾ cup milk and eggs. Dredge steaks in cracker crumb mixture; dip in milk mixture and dredge in cracker mixture again. Pour oil into a skillet; heat to 360 degrees. (Do not use a non-stick skillet.) Fry steaks in batches, about 15 minutes, turning once until golden. Remove to a wire rack on a sheet pan. Keep steaks warm in a 225 degree oven. Carefully drain hot oil, reserving cooked bits and one tablespoon drippings in skillet. Whisk together remaining ¼ cup flour, one teaspoon salt, one teaspoon pepper and 4 cups milk. Pour mixture into reserved drippings in skillet; cook over medium-high heat, whisking constantly, 10 to 12 minutes or until thickened. Serve gravy with steaks and mashed potatoes.

Chicken-Fried Steak

Carla Slajchert, *St. Petersburg, FL*

Mom's Cola Chicken

Growing up, we knew Mom would be making this delicious, tender chicken whenever we saw her get out the electric skillet.

Serves 4

1 to 2 T. oil
1½ lbs. boneless, skinless chicken breasts
salt and pepper to taste
20-oz. bottle cola, divided
1 to 2 c. catsup, divided

Heat oil in a large skillet over medium heat. Add chicken to oil; sprinkle with salt and pepper and brown on both sides. Pour enough cola into skillet to cover chicken. Slowly add enough catsup to skillet until mixture reaches desired thicknesss. Cover and cook over medium heat for about 45 minutes, adding remaining cola and catsup, a little at a time, every 10 to 15 minutes, until chicken juices run clear.

Ginny Schneider, *Muenster, TX*

Fried Green Tomatoes

Summer squash or okra can also be prepared using this same batter.

Serves 4

1 c. all-purpose flour
1 c. cornmeal
½ t. salt
½ t. pepper
3 green tomatoes, sliced
oil for frying

Whisk together dry ingredients. Dip tomatoes into mixture. Pour oil to a depth of 2 inches in a Dutch oven or cast-iron skillet; heat to 350 degrees. Fry tomatoes until golden and crisp on both sides.

～ Savvy Side ～

Serve creamed corn with fried green tomatoes for a great veggie combination. Blend 2 cups milk, 2 tablespoons flour and 2 tablespoons melted butter. Cook until thickened. Add 2 cups frozen or fresh corn, salt and pepper and bring to a boil. Yummy!

Fried Green Tomatoes

Dana Harpster, *Kansas City, MO*

Green Peas with Crispy Bacon

Rather than chase little round peas around the plate, be sure to serve this side with biscuits, or "pea pushers," to help you get every pea on your fork.

Serves 6

2 slices bacon
1 shallot, sliced
½ t. orange zest
½ c. fresh orange juice
¼ t. salt
½ t. pepper
16-oz. pkg. frozen sweet green peas, thawed
1 t. butter
1 T. fresh mint, chopped
Garnish: fresh mint sprigs

Cook bacon in a skillet over medium heat until crisp; remove and drain on paper towels, reserving one teaspoon drippings in skillet. Crumble bacon and set aside.

Sauté shallot in hot bacon drippings over medium-high heat for 2 minutes or until tender. Stir in orange zest, orange juice, salt and pepper. Cook, stirring occasionally, for 5 minutes or until reduced by half. Add peas and cook 5 more minutes; stir in butter and chopped mint. Transfer peas to a serving dish and sprinkle with crumbled bacon. Garnish as desired.

Tara Horton, *Delaware, OH*

Chicken Pesto Primo

One summer I grew basil in my garden and froze batches of homemade pesto in ice cube trays. I made up this recipe to use that yummy pesto. When asparagus isn't in season, I'll toss in some broccoli flowerets...it's just as tasty!

Serves 4

8-oz. pkg. rotini pasta, uncooked
2 c. cooked chicken, cubed
1 c. asparagus, steamed and cut into 1-inch
    pieces
2 T. basil pesto sauce
¼ to ½ c. chicken broth

Cook pasta according to package directions; drain. In a skillet over medium heat, combine chicken, asparagus, pesto, cooked pasta and ¼ cup chicken broth. Cook and stir until heated through, adding more broth as needed.

Chicken Pesto Primo

Melissa Hart, *Middleville, MI*

Zucchini Fritters

Here's a tasty way to get your family to eat their vegetables and use the surplus zucchini from your garden!

Serves 6

2 zucchini, grated (about 3½ c.)
1 egg
⅔ c. shredded Cheddar cheese
⅔ c. round buttery crackers, crumbled
½ t. salt
2 T. oil

Combine zucchini, egg, cheese, crackers and salt in a large mixing bowl. If mixture seems wet, add extra crackers; shape mixture into patties. Heat oil in a skillet; fry patties for about 3 minutes on each side or until golden brown.

Bev Fisher, *Mesa, AZ*

Grilled Havarti Sandwiches

Now that my children are grown, I'm always looking for recipes that call for ingredients they wouldn't eat. This sandwich is so tasty, I wanted another one the next day after I first tried it!

Makes 4 sandwiches

8 slices French bread
2 t. butter, softened and divided
4 T. apricot preserves
¼ lb. Havarti cheese, sliced
1 avocado, halved, pitted and sliced

Spread 4 slices bread on one side with half the butter and all the preserves. Top with cheese, avocado and another slice of bread; spread remaining butter on outside of sandwiches. Heat a large skillet over medium heat. Cook sandwiches for 2 to 3 minutes, until bread is golden and cheese begins to melt. Turn over; press down slightly with a spatula. Cook until golden.

⚍ Kitchen Tip ⚍

To keep vegetables fresh and nutritious, wrap them in paper towels and store in unsealed plastic bags in the refrigerator.

Grilled Havarti Sandwiches

Gail Blain, *Grand Island, NE*

Ham Steak & Apples Skillet

My grandmother's old black cast-iron skillet brings back wonderful memories of the delicious things she used to make in it. I seek out scrumptious skillet recipes just so I can use Grandma's old skillet...this one is a real family favorite.

Serves 6

3 T. butter
½ c. brown sugar, packed
1 T. Dijon mustard
2 c. apples, cored and diced
2 1-lb. bone-in ham steaks

Melt butter in a large skillet over medium heat. Add brown sugar and mustard; bring to a simmer. Add apples; cover and simmer for 5 minutes. Top apples with ham steaks. Cover with a lid; simmer for about 10 more minutes or until apples are tender. Remove ham to a platter and cut into serving-size pieces. Top ham with apples and sauce.

Roberta Goll, *Chesterfield, MI*

Roberta's Pepper Steak

This beef dish is as beautiful as it is yummy. I like to serve it right from the cast-iron skillet that I cook it in. Everyone always comments on it and wants the recipe!

Makes 8 servings

1¼ lbs. beef round steak, sliced into
    ½-inch strips
2 t. canola oil
2 cloves garlic, pressed and divided
2 green and/or red peppers, cut into thin strips
2 onions, coarsely chopped
8-oz. pkg. sliced mushrooms
½ t. salt
½ t. pepper
1 c. beef broth

In a skillet over medium heat, brown steak strips with oil and half the garlic. Add peppers and onions; cook until tender. Stir in mushrooms, salt, pepper and remaining garlic. Stir in beef broth. Reduce heat to low and simmer for one hour. Add a little water if needed.

Roberta's Pepper Steak

Ruth Cooksey, *Plainfield, IN*

Ruth's Swiss Bacon-Onion Dip

A yummy hot appetizer to serve with your favorite snack crackers.

Makes 4 cups

8 slices bacon
8-oz. pkg. cream cheese, softened
1 c. shredded Swiss cheese
1/2 c. mayonnaise
2 T. green onions, chopped
1 c. round buttery crackers, crushed

In a cast-iron skillet over medium-high heat, cook bacon until crisp. Remove bacon to paper towels. Drain skillet and wipe clean. Mix cheeses, mayonnaise and onion; spread in same skillet. Top with crumbled bacon and cracker crumbs. Transfer skillet to oven. Bake, uncovered, at 350 degrees for 15 to 20 minutes, until hot and bubbly.

Jack Johnson, *Kansas City, MO*

Dixie Fried Chicken

Fried chicken is comfort food at its best! And this crispy Southern-style chicken, complete with a creamy gravy, doesn't disappoint.

Serves 4

2 1/2 to 3-lb. broiler-fryer chicken, cut up, or
   2 1/2 lbs. assorted chicken pieces
1/2 t. salt
1/2 t. freshly ground pepper
1 1/2 c. all-purpose flour
1 t. cayenne pepper
1 egg, lightly beaten
1/3 c. milk
oil for frying

Season chicken with salt and pepper. Combine flour and cayenne pepper; set aside. Combine egg and milk; dip chicken in egg mixture and dredge in flour mixture, coating chicken well. Pour oil to a depth of one inch in a heavy skillet; heat oil to 350 degrees. Fry chicken in hot oil over medium heat for 15 to 20 minutes or until golden, turning occasionally. Remove small pieces earlier, if necessary, to prevent overbrowning. Drain chicken on paper towels, reserving 1/4 cup drippings in skillet for Cream Gravy. Serve with gravy.

CREAM GRAVY:

1/4 c. reserved pan drippings
1/4 c. all-purpose flour
2 1/2 to 3 c. hot milk
1/2 t. salt
1/4 t. freshly ground pepper
1/8 t. cayenne pepper

Heat pan drippings in skillet over medium heat. Add flour, stirring until browned. Gradually add hot milk; cook, stirring constantly, until thick and bubbly. Add salt, pepper and cayenne pepper. Serve hot. Makes 2 3/4 cups.

Dixie Fried Chicken

Lauren Vanden Berg, *Grandville, MI*

Skillet Meatloaf

My great-grandma was very poor and only owned one cast-iron skillet. She made this meatloaf in the skillet. She passed her skillet on to my grandma, who passed it on to me. Now this is the only kind of meatloaf I make.

Serves 3 to 4

1 lb. ground beef
1 onion, chopped
1 green pepper, chopped
4 saltine crackers, crushed
1-oz. pkg. ranch salad dressing mix
1 egg
¼ c. barbecue sauce

In a bowl, combine beef, onion and green pepper; mix well. Add cracker crumbs and dressing mix; mix again. Shape beef mixture into ball; make a little hole in the middle. Crack the egg into the hole; mix again. Preheat a cast-iron skillet or 3 to 4 individual skillets over medium heat. Shape meatloaf to fit in skillet(s). Add meatloaf to skillet(s). Spread barbecue sauce on top. Cover and cook for 30 to 35 minutes for a large skillet or 20 to 25 minutes for smaller skillets, until meatloaf is no longer pink in the center. Reduce heat to low, if needed. Use a meat thermometer to check temperature if desired; internal temperature should be 160 degrees.

J.J. Presley, *Portland, TX*

Cheesy Sausage-Potato Casserole

Add some fresh green beans too, if you like.

Serves 6 to 8

3 to 4 potatoes, sliced
2 8-oz. links pork sausage, sliced into
   2-inch lengths
1 onion, chopped
½ c. butter, sliced
1 c. shredded Cheddar cheese

Layer potatoes, sausage and onion in a skillet sprayed with non-stick vegetable spray. Dot with butter; sprinkle with cheese. Bake at 350 degrees for 1½ hours.

Cheesy Sausage-Potato Casserole

Jill Ross, *Pickerington, OH*

Kale & Potato Casserole

Warm potatoes, wilted greens and Parmesan cheese make this a hearty side!

Serves 4 to 6

1/4 c. butter, melted
3 potatoes, thinly sliced
10 leaves fresh kale, finely chopped
5 T. grated Parmesan cheese
salt and pepper to taste

Drizzle melted butter over potatoes in a bowl; mix well. In a greased cast-iron skillet layer 1/3 each of potatoes, kale and Parmesan cheese; season with s alt and pepper. Continue layering and seasoning, ending with cheese. Cover skillet and transfer to oven. Bake at 375 degrees for 30 minutes. Uncover; bake for another 15 to 30 minutes, until potatoes are tender.

Charlie Tuggle, *Palo Alto, CA*

Chicken Enchilada Nacho Bowls

Your family will love this combination of hot and cold all in one bowl.

Serves 4

1 onion, diced
1 T. olive oil
10-oz. can enchilada sauce
1 c. canned crushed tomatoes
15 1/2-oz. can black beans, drained and rinsed
1 t. dried oregano
1 T. brown sugar, packed
2 c. rotisserie chicken, shredded
8-oz. pkg. tortilla or corn chips, coarsely crushed
1 1/4 c. shredded Cheddar cheese
2 c. lettuce, shredded
1/4 c. fresh cilantro, chopped
Garnish: 4 lime slices
Optional: hot pepper sauce

In a skillet over medium-high heat, sauté onion in oil until softened. Add enchilada sauce, tomatoes, beans, oregano and sugar; cook, stirring occasionally, until hot and slightly cooked down, about 5 minutes. Stir in chicken; cook until warmed through. To serve, divide chips among 4 bowls; top with chicken mixture, cheese, lettuce and cilantro. Serve with lime slices and hot sauce, if desired.

Chicken Enchilada Nacho Bowls

Brenda Derby, *Northborough, MA*

Apple-Cranberry Crisp

We like to make this using several different varieties of tart baking apples.

Serves 10 to 12

6 c. apples, peeled, cored and sliced
3 c. cranberries
1 c. sugar
2 t. cinnamon
1 to 2 t. lemon juice
¾ c. butter, sliced and divided
1 c. all-purpose flour
1 c. brown sugar, packed
Garnish: vanilla ice cream

Toss together apple slices, cranberries, sugar and cinnamon. Spread in a greased skillet. Sprinkle with lemon juice and dot with ¼ cup butter. Blend remaining butter with flour and brown sugar until crumbly; sprinkle over apple mixture. Bake at 350 degrees for one hour. Serve warm with vanilla ice cream.

Jodi Rhodes, *Tolland, CT*

Whole-Wheat Pumpkin Skillet Cake

This scrumptious recipe came out of the desire for a healthier cake. For a real show-stopper, top it with freshly whipped cream.

Makes 8 servings

¼ c. butter, sliced
½ c. brown sugar, packed
1 egg, beaten
½ t. vanilla extract
½ ripe banana, mashed
⅓ c. canned pumpkin
1 c. whole-wheat flour
½ t. baking soda
¼ t. salt
½ t. cinnamon
¼ t. nutmeg
½ c. chopped walnuts
½ c. semi-sweet chocolate chips

Melt butter in a 9" cast-iron skillet over medium heat. Remove from heat; stir in brown sugar. Let cool. Whisk in egg; stir in vanilla. Add mashed banana and pumpkin; stir until blended and set aside. In a bowl, combine flour, baking soda, salt and spices. Add to pumpkin mixture in skillet; stir until well mixed. Stir in walnuts and chocolate chips; smooth top with spoon. Bake at 350 degrees for 15 to 20 minutes. Cut into wedges to serve.

Whole-Wheat Pumpkin Skillet Cake

Joanne Nagle, *Ashtabula, OH*

Country-Style Skillet Apples

This recipe has been in my family for years and years. Using a cast-iron skillet makes it seem authentic...like it was also enjoyed many years ago.

Makes 6 servings

3 T. butter
3 T. sugar
½ t. cinnamon
2 T. cornstarch
1 c. water
4 Golden Delicious apples, peeled, cored and sliced

Melt butter in a skillet over medium heat. Stir in sugar, cinnamon and cornstarch; mix well and stir in water. Add apple slices. Cook over medium heat, stirring until thick and apples are tender.

Shelley Turner, *Boise, ID*

Eva's Fruit Cobbler

The combination of rhubarb and strawberries is a classic and oh-so-yummy in this dessert.

Makes 8 servings

4 c. rhubarb, sliced
4 c. strawberries, hulled and halved
1 c. sugar, divided
¼ c. water
2 T. apple juice
1 T. cornstarch
1 c. all-purpose flour
1 t. baking powder
¼ t. baking soda
¼ t. salt
¼ c. butter
½ c. buttermilk
½ t. almond extract
Garnish: 2 t. coarse sugar

In a large, oven-safe skillet, combine fruit, ¾ cup sugar and water; bring to a boil. Reduce heat, cover and simmer for 10 minutes. Combine apple juice and cornstarch in a container with a tight-fitting lid; shake well to blend. Stir into fruit and cook until mixture thickens. Keep warm. Combine remaining dry ingredients, including remaining sugar, in a bowl. Cut in butter with a pastry blender or 2 forks until mixture resembles crumbs. Stir together buttermilk and extract; add to dough. Stir to blend well and drop by tablespoonfuls onto hot fruit. Sprinkle with coarse sugar. Bake at 400 degrees for 20 minutes, or until golden.

Eva's Fruit Cobbler

Muffin Tin Recipes

Muffin tins have been around for a long time and can be found in aluminum, graniteware, ceramic and even cast iron. They can be large or tiny cups that contain just the right portion of whatever goodie they hold. These little treasures are perfect for muffins and cupcakes, but they can also be used for savory meat and egg dishes. For a breakfast treat try Mini Ham & Swiss Frittatas or Maple Ham & Egg Cups. Everyone loves muffins and our Speedy Sausage Muffins and Carroty Bran Muffins won't disappoint! Muffin Tin Meatloaves make the perfect main dish, with Kathy's Bacon Popovers on the side. Need a showy dessert that everyone will love? Try Taffy Apple Cupcakes and Pineapple Upside-Down Cupcakes for that perfect sweet treat. So grab those muffin tins and fill them up with the perfect recipe for your family & friends to enjoy.

Jeanne Barringer, *Edgewater, FL*

Sour Cream Mini Biscuits

Once you start snacking on these little gems, it's hard to stop!

Makes 4 dozen

1 c. butter, softened
1 c. sour cream
2 c. self-rising flour

Blend butter and sour cream together until fluffy; gradually mix in flour. Drop by teaspoonfuls into greased mini muffin tins; bake at 450 degrees for 10 to 12 minutes.

Maria Temple, *New York, NY*

Sugar-Topped Muffins

Enjoy these warm muffins for a real treat!

Makes 2 dozen

18¼-oz. pkg. white cake mix
1 c. milk
2 eggs
½ t. nutmeg
⅓ c. sugar
½ t. cinnamon
¼ c. butter, melted

Blend cake mix, milk, eggs and nutmeg at low speed with an electric mixer until just moistened; beat at high speed 2 minutes. Fill paper-lined muffin cups ⅔ full. Bake at 350 degrees until golden, about 15 to 18 minutes. Cool 5 minutes. Combine sugar and cinnamon on a small plate. Brush muffin tops with butter; roll in sugar and cinnamon mixture. Serve warm.

Beckie Apple, *Grannis, AR*

Speedy Sausage Muffins

Serve these for breakfast, lunch or for a snack.

Makes 16 muffins

1 lb. ground pork sausage, browned and drained
3 c. biscuit baking mix
1½ c. shredded Cheddar cheese
10¾-oz. can Cheddar cheese soup
¾ c. water

Combine sausage, baking mix and cheese in a large bowl; make a well in center of mixture. Stir together soup and water; add to sausage mixture, stirring just until combined. Spoon into lightly greased muffin cups, filling to top of cups. Bake at 375 degrees for 20 to 25 minutes, until lightly golden. Serve warm.

Speedy Sausage Muffins

Laura Parker, *Flagstaff, AZ*

My Mom's Muffin Donuts

These are a big treat anytime, so keep a few in the freezer to warm up for a quick and special breakfast!

Makes one dozen

2 c. all-purpose flour
½ t. salt
1 T. baking powder
½ t. nutmeg
½ c. plus ½ t. butter, divided
1½ c. sugar, divided
1 egg, beaten
¾ c. milk
¾ c. semi-sweet chocolate chips
½ c. chopped pecans
2 t. cinnamon

Combine flour, salt, baking powder, nutmeg, ½ teaspoon butter, ½ cup sugar, egg and milk. Fold in chocolate chips and pecans. Fill greased muffin cups ⅔ full. Bake at 350 degrees for 20 minutes. Remove immediately from pan. Melt the remaining butter; roll muffins in butter. Combine remaining sugar and cinnamon; roll muffins in mixture.

Meri Herbert, *Cheboygan, MI*

Carroty Bran Muffins

These muffins have so much texture and flavor and stay moist. Keep them refrigerated after baking to keep them fresh.

Makes 16 large muffins

2½ c. all-purpose flour
2½ c. bran cereal
1½ c. sugar
2½ t. baking soda
1 t. salt
2 c. buttermilk
⅓ c. applesauce
2 eggs, beaten
1½ c. carrots, peeled and shredded
1 green apple, cored and chopped
1 c. sweetened dried cranberries
½ c. chopped walnuts
¼ c. ground flax seed

Mix all ingredients together in a large bowl. Cover and refrigerate batter for up to 2 days, or bake right away. Fill 16 large, greased muffin cups ⅔ full. Bake at 375 degrees for 15 to 18 minutes; do not overbake. Muffins will become moister if allowed to stand for awhile.

Carroty Bran Muffins

Donna Meyer, *Pensacola, FL*

Sweet Apple Butter Muffins

Apple butter makes these moist and sweet.

Makes one dozen

1¾ c. all-purpose flour
⅓ c. plus 2 T. sugar, divided
2 t. baking powder
½ t. cinnamon
¼ t. nutmeg
¼ t. salt
1 egg, beaten
¾ c. milk
¼ c. oil
1 t. vanilla extract
⅓ c. apple butter
⅓ c. chopped pecans

Combine flour, ⅓ cup sugar, baking powder, spices and salt in a large bowl; set aside. In a separate bowl, blend egg, milk, oil and vanilla together; stir into flour mixture. Spoon one tablespoon batter into each of 12 paper-lined muffin cups; top with one teaspoon apple butter. Fill muffin cups ⅔ full using remaining batter; set aside. Toss pecans with remaining sugar; sprinkle evenly over muffins. Bake at 400 degrees until a toothpick inserted in the center tests clean, about 20 minutes.

Carol Field Dahlstrom, *Ankeny, IA*

Bacon-Corn Muffins

Little bits of crisp bacon make these muffins a breakfast favorite.

Makes 2 dozen

2¾ c. all-purpose flour
¾ c. sugar
⅔ c. cornmeal
1 t. salt
1 t. baking powder
½ t. baking soda
1 c. bacon, crisply cooked and cut or broken
    into ½-inch pieces
1½ c. buttermilk
4 eggs, beaten
¾ c. oil
⅔ c. shredded Cheddar cheese
¼ c. red or orange peppers, chopped

In a large bowl, combine flour, sugar, cornmeal, salt, baking powder, baking soda and bacon. Make a well in the dry ingredients. Set aside. In a small bowl, mix buttermilk, eggs and oil. Slowly pour egg mixture into flour mixture, stirring until just moistened. Fold in cheese and peppers. Spoon batter into 24 paper-lined or greased muffin cups, filling ¾ full. Bake at 375 degrees for 20 to 25 minutes, until golden and firm in the center.

Bacon-Corn Muffins

Staci Meyers, *Montezuma, GA*

Maple Ham & Egg Cups

Ham and eggs make such a great breakfast or brunch...the kids will love the novelty too.

Serves 6

1 T. butter, melted
6 slices deli baked ham
1 T. maple syrup
1 t. butter, cut into 6 pieces
6 eggs
salt and pepper to taste
English muffins, toast or biscuits

Brush muffin cups in pans with melted butter; line each cup with a slice of ham. Pour ½ teaspoon maple syrup over each ham slice; top with one pat of butter. Crack one egg into each ham cup; season with salt and pepper as desired. Bake at 400 degrees for 20 minutes or until eggs are set. Remove muffin cups from oven; use a spoon or gently twist each serving to loosen. Serve on English muffins, with toast or on split biscuits.

Celestina Torrez, *Camden, NJ*

Mini Ham & Swiss Frittatas

I first started making these for my toddlers as easy-to-handle mini omelets. My husband thought they would be yummy as appetizers too, so now I serve them when we're watching the big game on TV. They're still a hit with my kids too!

Makes 2 dozen

8-oz. pkg. cooked ham, diced
⅔ c. shredded Swiss cheese
¼ c. fresh chives, chopped
pepper to taste
8 eggs, beaten

In a bowl, mix together ham, cheese, chives and pepper; set aside. Spray mini muffin cups with non-stick vegetable spray. Fill muffin cups half full with cheese mixture. Spoon in eggs to fill cups. Bake at 375 degrees until golden, about 13 minutes. Serve warm.

Mini Ham & Swiss Frittatas

Melissa Mishler, *Columbia City, IN*

Cream Cheese-Filled Cupcakes

These are so delicious, you might want to make a double batch!

Makes about 2 dozen

18¼-oz. pkg. German chocolate cake mix
1 c. mini semi-sweet chocolate chips
⅓ c. sugar
1 egg, beaten
8-oz. pkg. cream cheese, softened

Prepare cake mix according to package directions. Fill paper-lined muffin cups ½ full. Combine remaining ingredients; drop by teaspoonfuls onto batter. Bake at 350 degrees for 20 to 25 minutes. Cool completely.

Kathy Murphy, *Lawrence, NE*

Peanut Butter Cup Cupcakes

I serve these at Sunday morning coffee time at church. Everyone loves them. There are never any leftovers!

Makes 16

⅓ c. butter, softened
⅓ c. creamy peanut butter
1¼ c. brown sugar, packed
2 eggs, beaten
1 t. vanilla extract
1¾ c. all-purpose flour
1¾ t. baking powder

1 t. salt
1 c. milk
16 mini peanut butter cups

In a bowl, combine butter, peanut butter and brown sugar. Beat in eggs and vanilla. Combine flour, baking powder and salt; add to butter mixture alternately with milk. Fill paper-lined muffin cups half full. Press a peanut butter cup into the center of each, until top edge is even with batter. Bake at 350 degrees for 22 to 24 minutes, until a toothpick inserted on an angle toward the center tests clean. Cool in tin on wire rack 10 minutes. Remove from tin and cool completely.

Kathy Grashoff, *Fort Wayne, IN*

Kathy's Bacon Popovers

Mmm...bacon! Serve these tasty popovers with a salad for a dinner they'll love.

Makes one dozen

2 eggs
1 c. milk
1 T. oil
1 c. all-purpose flour
½ t. salt
3 slices bacon, crisply cooked and crumbled

Whisk together eggs, milk and oil. Beat in flour and salt just until smooth. Fill 12 greased and floured muffin cups ⅔ full. Sprinkle bacon evenly over batter. Bake at 400 degrees for 25 to 30 minutes, until until puffed and golden. Serve warm.

Kathy's Bacon Popovers

Geneva Rogers, *Gillette, WY*

Orange-Glazed Chocolate Rolls

What a treat. The entire family loves these!

Makes about 1¹⁄₂ dozen

3 c. all-purpose flour, divided
2 envs. active dry yeast
1 t. salt
1 t. cinnamon
1¹⁄₄ c. water
¹⁄₃ c. sugar
¹⁄₃ c. butter
1 egg
Optional: ¹⁄₂ c. raisins
1 c. semi-sweet chocolate chips

Stir together 1¹⁄₂ cups flour, yeast, salt and cinnamon in a large bowl. Combine water, sugar and butter in a saucepan over medium-low heat, stirring constantly until butter is almost melted (115 to 120 degrees). Add water mixture to flour mixture; blend until smooth. Mix in egg; stir in remaining flour. Fold in raisins, if desired; cover dough and let rise in a warm place (85 degrees), free from drafts, for one hour, until double in bulk. Punch down dough; let rest for 10 minutes. Fold in chocolate chips; fill greased muffin cups ²⁄₃ full. Cover; let rise until double in bulk. Bake at 425 degrees for 10 to 15 minutes, until golden. Glaze before serving.

GLAZE:

¹⁄₂ c. powdered sugar
3 t. orange juice

Combine sugar and juice in a small bowl; stir until smooth and creamy.

Trysha Mapley-Barron, *Wasilla, AK*

Sweet Avocado Muffins

These muffins are not too sweet and are so moist and good!

Makes one dozen

2 c. all-purpose flour
1 t. baking powder
1 t. baking soda
¹⁄₂ t. sea salt
2 eggs
1 c. sugar
¹⁄₂ c. canola oil
1¹⁄₂ c. very ripe avocado, halved, pitted
    and mashed
1 T. lime juice
1¹⁄₄ t. vanilla extract
Optional: ¹⁄₂ c. chopped walnuts

In a large bowl, mix together flour, baking powder, baking soda and salt; set aside. In a separate bowl, beat eggs and sugar until fluffy; stir in oil, avocado, lime juice and vanilla. Add oil mixture to flour mixture; stir just until combined. Spoon batter into 12 paper-lined muffin cups, filling ²⁄₃ full. Sprinkle with walnuts, if desired. Bake at 350 degrees for 15 to 20 minutes, until a toothpick inserted in center tests clean. Remove muffins to a wire rack; let cool.

Sweet Avocado Muffins

Lena Smith, *Pickerington, OH*

Key Lime Cupcakes

I spent the summer trying different-flavored cupcakes. I made these for our church's bake-off and won Honorable Mention!

Makes 2 dozen

16-oz. pkg. angel food cake mix
¾ c. lemon-lime soda
½ c. plus 1 T. Key lime juice, divided
14-oz. can sweetened condensed milk
1 t. lime zest
8-oz. container frozen whipped topping, thawed
Garnish: sweetened flaked coconut

In a large bowl, combine dry cake mix, soda and ¼ cup lime juice. Spray muffin cups with non-stick vegetable spray. Fill muffin cups ⅔ full. Bake at 350 degrees for 12 minutes, or until a toothpick tests clean. Cool completely. Use a toothpick to poke several holes almost to the bottom of each cupcake; don't poke through bottoms. Mix together remaining lime juice, sweetened condensed milk and lime zest. Measure out ⅓ cup lime mixture; pour over all the cupcake tops. Stir whipped topping into the remaining lime mixture; chill for one hour. Frost cupcakes with whipped topping mixture. Garnish with coconut. Refrigerate until serving time.

Kathy Dean, *Eau Claire, WI*

Muffin Tin Meatloaves

These little gems cook up super fast, almost twice as fast as a traditional meatloaf.

Makes 12 mini meatloaves

1½ lbs. lean ground beef
1 egg, lightly beaten
1 c. Italian-seasoned dry bread crumbs
1½ c. zucchini, shredded
½ t. salt
¼ c. catsup
Optional: dried parsley

In a large bowl, combine all ingredients except catsup and optional parsley. Mix lightly but thoroughly. Place ⅓ cup of beef mixture into each of 12 lightly greased muffin cups, pressing lightly. Spread catsup over tops. Sprinkle with dried parsley if desired. Bake at 400 degrees for 35 minutes, or until no pink remains and juices run clear.

~ **Quick Tip** ~

Garden-fresh herbs are delicious. If you have them on hand, just use double the amount of dried herbs called for in a recipe.

Muffin Tin Meatloaves

Angie Biggins, *Lyons, IL*

Taffy Apple Cupcakes

What fun...a gooey caramel-topped cupcake on a stick!

Makes one dozen

18¼-oz. pkg. carrot cake mix
1 c. Granny Smith apples, cored, peeled and
    finely chopped
½ t. cinnamon
20 caramels, unwrapped
¼ c. milk
1 c. pecans or walnuts, finely chopped
12 wooden craft sticks

Prepare cake mix according to package instructions; stir in apples and cinnamon. Fill paper-lined jumbo muffin cups ⅔ full. Bake at 350 degrees for 20 to 25 minutes, until a toothpick inserted near center tests clean. Combine caramels and milk in a small saucepan over low heat; stir until melted and smooth. Drizzle caramel over cooled cupcakes; sprinkle nuts over top. Insert a craft stick into center of each cupcake.

Judy Mitchell, *Huntley, IL*

Judy's Famous Banana Muffins

Our local newspaper featured me as "Cook of the Week" with this recipe! I found the original recipe many years ago and have revised it over the years. It's a favorite of family & friends.

Makes one dozen

3 very ripe bananas, mashed
2 eggs, beaten
½ c. canola oil
½ c. plus 1 T. sugar, divided
½ c. quick-cooking oats, uncooked
½ c. whole-wheat flour
½ c. all-purpose flour
½ c. wheat germ
1 t. vanilla extract
1 t. baking powder
½ t. baking soda
¼ t. salt
¼ c. chopped walnuts

In a large bowl, stir together bananas, eggs, oil and ½ cup sugar until combined. Add remaining ingredients except walnuts and remaining sugar; stir just until blended. Spoon batter into 12 paper-lined muffin cups, filling about ⅔ full. Sprinkle tops with walnuts and remaining sugar. Bake at 350 degrees for 20 to 25 minutes, until golden and a toothpick tests clean. Let muffins cool in tin for 5 minutes; remove to a wire rack and cool completely.

Judy's Famous Banana Muffins

Pat Smith, *Bonham, TX*

Frozen Apricot Salad

A refreshing salad for those hot summer days.

Serves 12

2 12-oz. pkgs. frozen strawberries, thawed
12-oz. can apricot pie filling
16½-oz. can pineapple tidbits, drained, and
    juice reserved
3 bananas, chopped
⅔ c. sugar

In a large bowl, mix together all ingredients until
sugar is dissolved. Pour mixture evenly into
muffin cups. Place in freezer for at least 4 hours.
Remove from freezer 15 minutes before serving.

Vickie, *Gooseberry Patch*

Mini Mousse Cupcakes

*Chocolate lovers will swoon over these
delectable cakes!*

Makes about 2 dozen

2⅓ c. milk chocolate chips
6 eggs, beaten
¼ c. plus 2 T. all-purpose flour
Garnish: whipped cream, chocolate shavings

Melt chocolate in a double boiler over medium
heat and let cool slightly. In a large bowl, beat
eggs and flour. Beat in melted chocolate until

combined. Fill paper-lined mini muffin cups
⅔ full. Bake at 325 degrees for 7 to 10 minutes, until
edges are done and centers shake slightly. Cool in
tin on wire rack for 20 minutes. Remove from tin;
cool completely. Garnish with whipped cream and
chocolate shavings.

Corinne Gross, *Tigard, OR*

Grandma's Tomato Muffins

*These savory muffins go great with almost any
soup and take just a few minutes to make!*

Makes one dozen

1 c. all-purpose flour
1 c. whole-wheat flour
¼ c. grated Parmesan cheese
2 T. sugar
1 T. baking powder
¼ t. salt
½ t. dried oregano
1 egg, beaten
1 c. buttermilk
⅓ c. butter, melted
1 ripe tomato, coarsely chopped
3 T. shredded Parmesan cheese

In a bowl, combine flours, cheese, sugar, baking
powder, salt and oregano. Mix well. Stir in egg,
buttermilk and butter just until blended. Fold in
tomato. Spoon batter into 12 paper-lined muffin
cups, filling ¾ full. Sprinkle with cheese. Bake at
400 degrees for about 15 minutes.

Grandma's Tomato Muffins

Robin Hill, *Rochester, NY*

Easiest Boston Cream Cupcakes

My most-requested muffin-like cupcakes!

Makes 2 dozen

18¼-oz. pkg. yellow cake mix
3.4-oz. pkg. instant vanilla pudding mix
1 c. cold milk
1½ c. frozen whipped topping, thawed and
   divided
4 1-oz. sqs. semi-sweet baking chocolate

Prepare cake mix according to package directions. Fill greased muffin cups ⅔ full and bake at 350 degrees for 15 to 20 minutes. Cool completely. Whisk pudding mix and milk for 2 minutes; let stand 5 minutes. Use a serrated knife to cut off the top of each cupcake; set tops aside. Stir ½ cup whipped topping into pudding. Spoon one tablespoon onto each cupcake; replace cupcake tops. In a microwave-safe bowl, combine remaining whipped topping and chocolate. Microwave for one minute; stir and microwave an additional 30 seconds. Stir until chocolate is melted; let stand 15 minutes. Frost cupcakes with chocolate mixture.

Bonnie Allard, *Santa Rosa, CA*

Peach Cobbler Cupcakes

These cupcakes are sweet because of the canned peaches, so they don't need frosting. So easy!

Makes 1½ dozen

3 c. all-purpose flour
1 c. sugar
1½ T. baking soda
½ t. salt
¾ c. butter, diced
1¾ c. milk
15-oz. can sliced peaches, drained and chopped
Optional: 6 T. brown sugar, packed

Mix flour, sugar, baking soda and salt in a large bowl. Cut in butter with a pastry blender or a fork. Add milk and peaches; stir just until moistened. Spoon batter into 18 greased muffin cups, filling ⅔ full. Add one teaspoon of brown sugar into the center of each cupcake, if desired. Bake at 400 degrees for 15 to 20 minutes, until golden. Turn out and cool slightly on a wire rack; serve warm or cooled.

Peach Cobbler Cupcakes

Kerry Mayer, *Dunham Springs, LA*

Toasted Coconut Cupcakes

My sister, Vanessa, made these amazing cupcakes for a church bake sale and they were a tremendous success.

Makes one dozen

8-oz. pkg. white cake mix
1 t. cinnamon
⅓ c. butter, softened
1 c. sugar
1 egg, beaten
1 t. vanilla extract
¾ c. milk

Combine dry cake mix and cinnamon in a bowl; set aside. Blend butter and sugar; mix in egg and vanilla. Beat into the cake mixture alternately with milk. Fill paper-lined muffin cups half full. Bake at 350 degrees for 20 to 25 minutes. Let cool slightly. While cupcakes are warm in the tin, spread 2 teaspoons Coconut Frosting onto the center of each; don't spread to edges. Broil cupcakes in tin until coconut is lightly toasted, about 2 to 3 minutes.

COCONUT FROSTING:

¼ c. butter, softened
⅓ c. brown sugar, packed
2 T. milk
1 c. sweetened flaked coconut
1 t. cinnamon

Combine butter and brown sugar. Blend in remaining ingredients.

Sharon Tillman, *Hampton, VA*

Pineapple Upside-Down Cupcakes

These little pineapple beauties are always a special treat. The kids ask for them all the time!

Makes 12 cupcakes

20-oz. can pineapple tidbits, drained and
 ½ c. juice reserved
⅓ c. brown sugar, packed
⅓ c. butter, melted
1 c. all-purpose flour
¾ c. sugar
½ t. baking powder
¼ c. butter, softened
1 egg, beaten
Garnish: maraschino cherries

Pat pineapple dry with paper towels. In a bowl, combine brown sugar and melted butter; divide mixture evenly into 12 greased muffin cups. Arrange pineapple chunks over brown sugar mixture. In a bowl, combine flour, sugar and baking powder. Mix in softened butter and reserved pineapple juice; beat for 2 minutes. Beat in egg. Spoon batter over pineapple, filling each cup ¾ full. Bake at 350 degrees for 30 minutes, or until a toothpick tests clean. Cool in pan for 5 minutes. Place a wire rack on top of muffin tin and invert cupcakes onto rack so pineapple is on top. Cool completely and top each with a cherry.

Pineapple Upside-Down Cupcakes

Bernadette Dobias, *Houston, TX*

Emma's Gingerbread Muffins

These little gingerbread gems are great to serve during the holidays, but we like them any time of year!

Makes 2½ dozen

½ c. butter, softened
½ c. shortening
¾ c. sugar
3 eggs
½ c. molasses
¼ c. light corn syrup
3 c. all-purpose flour
2 t. cinnamon
2 t. ground ginger
1 t. nutmeg
1 t. baking soda
1 c. buttermilk

Combine butter and shortening in a large bowl. Beat with an electric mixer at medium speed until creamy. Add sugar; beat just until combined. Add eggs, one at a time, beating after each addition. Add molasses and corn syrup; beat just until blended. Sift together flour and spices. Dissolve baking soda in buttermilk; add the milk mixture to butter mixture alternately with flour mixture, stirring just until combined. Fill greased and floured muffin cups ⅔ full. Bake at 350 degrees for 15 minutes, or until a toothpick inserted in center comes out clean.

Amy Tucker, *British Columbia, Canada*

Peanut Butter Muffins

These will become your family's favorite muffins. They are so moist and full of peanut-buttery flavor!

Makes 1½ dozen

1 c. whole-wheat flour
1 c. long-cooking oats, uncooked
1½ t. baking soda
¼ c. creamy peanut butter
⅓ c. applesauce
1½ c. milk
¼ c. honey
2 T. finely chopped peanuts

Whisk together flour, oats and baking soda. Add peanut butter and applesauce; beat with an electric mixer on low speed until smooth. Stir in milk and honey. Spoon batter into paper-lined or greased muffin cups, filling two-thirds full. Sprinkle with chopped peanuts. Bake at 350 degrees for 12 to 15 minutes, until a toothpick tests clean. Cool in pan 5 minutes; transfer to a wire rack to finish cooling.

Peanut Butter Muffins

Kathy Grashoff, *Fort Wayne, IN*

Brie Kisses

These make such a great addition to a holiday plate of cookies.

Makes 32

²/₃ lb. Brie cheese
17.3-oz. pkg. frozen puff pastry
Garnish: red or green hot pepper jelly

Cut Brie into 32 ½-inch cubes; arrange on a plate and place in the freezer. Let pastry thaw at room temperature 30 minutes; unfold each pastry and roll with a rolling pin to remove creases. Slice each sheet into quarters; slice each quarter in half. Cut each piece in half one more time for a total of 32 squares. Place squares into greased mini muffin cups; arrange so corners of dough point upward. Bake at 400 degrees for 5 minutes. Place one Brie cube in center of each pastry. Bake 10 minutes or until edges are golden. Remove from pan. Immediately top with pepper jelly.

Sonna Johnson, *Goldfield, IA*

Cranberry Applesauce Muffins

I like to make these by the dozen and take them to church for after-church coffee.

Makes 2 dozen

1 c. fresh or frozen cranberries
1¼ c. unsweetened applesauce
⅓ c. canola oil
1 egg, beaten
2 c. all-purpose flour
½ c. sugar
1 t. baking soda
1 t. cinnamon
½ t. salt

Using a food processor, process cranberries until chopped. Set aside. In a small bowl, mix applesauce, oil and egg. In a large bowl, combine flour, sugar, baking soda, cinnamon and salt. Make a well in the flour mixture. Slowly pour in applesauce mixture, stirring until just moistened. Fold in cranberries. Fill 24 greased or paper-lined muffin cups ²/₃ full. Bake at 350 degrees for 25 to 30 minutes, until a wooden toothpick inserted in the center comes out clean. Cool for 2 minutes before removing from cups.

Cranberry Applesauce Muffins

Diana Bulls, *Reedley, CA*

Snickerdoodle Cupcakes

An easy and delicious version of an all-time favorite cookie!

Makes one dozen

18¼-oz. pkg. white cake mix
1 c. milk
½ c. butter, melted and cooled slightly
3 eggs, beaten
1 t. vanilla extract
2 t. cinnamon

In a large bowl, combine dry cake mix and remaining ingredients. Beat with an electric mixer on low speed for 3 minutes. Fill greased muffin cups ⅔ full. Bake at 350 degrees for 22 to 25 minutes. Let cool. Frost with Cinnamon Frosting.

CINNAMON FROSTING:

½ c. butter, softened
1 t. vanilla extract
1 T. cinnamon
3¾ c. powdered sugar
3 to 4 T. milk

Beat butter until fluffy. Mix in vanilla, cinnamon and powdered sugar. Stir in enough milk for desired consistency.

Kelly Marshall, *Olathe, KS*

Kelly's Easy Caramel Rolls

This is a much-requested family recipe! Serve with a fresh fruit salad for a special brunch.

3 T. corn syrup, divided
3 T. brown sugar, packed and divided
3 T. chopped pecans, divided
2 T. butter, cubed and divided
12-oz. tube refrigerated biscuits

To each of 10 greased muffin cups, add one teaspoon each of syrup, brown sugar and pecans. Top each with ½ teaspoon butter and one biscuit. Bake at 400 degrees for 8 to 10 minutes, until golden. Invert rolls onto a plate before serving.

Kelly's Easy Caramel Rolls

Janis Parr, *Ontario, Canada*

Butterfly Yeast Rolls

I have been baking these delicious rolls for years, and they are the best! The rolls rise to perfection and are golden and flaky...sure to delight family & friends.

Makes one dozen

1 env. active dry yeast
¼ c. warm water
1 c. milk
¼ c. sugar
¼ c. shortening
1 t. salt
3½ c. all-purpose flour, divided
1 egg, beaten

Dissolve yeast in warm water (110 to 115 degrees) in a small bowl; let stand for 5 minutes. Heat milk in a small saucepan over low heat just until boiling; let cool slightly. Combine milk, sugar, shortening and salt in a large bowl. Add 1½ cups flour and beat well. Beat in yeast mixture and egg. Gradually knead in remaining flour to form a soft dough. Place in a greased bowl, turning once. Cover and let rise in a warm place for 2 hours. Punch dough down; turn out on a floured surface. Shape into 36 walnut-size balls; place 3 balls in each cup of a greased muffin tin. Cover and let rise for 45 minutes. Bake at 400 degrees for 12 to 15 minutes, until golden.

Lillian Dahlstrom, *Ames, IA*

Maple-Walnut Muffins

These are super yummy muffins that our entire family loves...and they are gluten-free!

Makes 1½ dozen

1 c. buckwheat flour
1 c. tapioca flour
1 t. baking soda
¼ t. salt
½ c. rice bran
2 bananas, mashed
⅔ c. buttermilk
½ c. real maple syrup
¼ c. oil
1 egg, beaten
⅔ c. walnuts

In a large bowl, mix buckwheat flour, tapioca flour, baking soda and salt. Add rice bran and mix well. Make a well in flour mixture. Set aside. In a medium bowl, mix bananas, buttermilk, maple syrup, oil and egg. Slowly pour banana mixture into flour mixture. Stir until just moistened. Fold in walnuts. Fill 18 greased muffin cups ⅔ full. Bake at 350 degrees for about 20 minutes, until a toothpick inserted in the center comes out clean.

Maple-Walnut Muffins

Index

Index

U.S. to Metric Recipe Equivalents

Volume Measurements

¼ teaspoon . . . . 1 mL
½ teaspoon . . . . 2 mL
1 teaspoon . . . . 5 mL
1 tablespoon = 3 teaspoons . . . . 15 mL
2 tablespoons = 1 fluid ounce . . . . 30 mL
¼ cup . . . . 60 mL
⅓ cup . . . . 75 mL
½ cup = 4 fluid ounces . . . . 125 mL
1 cup = 8 fluid ounces . . . . 250 mL
2 cups = 1 pint = 16 fluid ounces . . 500 mL
4 cups = 1 quart . . . . 1 L

Weights

1 ounce . . . . 30 g
4 ounces . . . . 120 g
8 ounces . . . . 225 g
16 ounces = 1 pound . . . . 450 g

Baking Pan Sizes

Square

8x8x2 inches . . . . 2 L = 20x20x5 cm
9x9x2 inches . . . . 2.5 L = 23x23x5 cm

Rectangular

13x9x2 inches . . . . 3.5 L = 33x23x5 cm

Loaf

9x5x3 inches . . . . 2 L = 23x13x7 cm

Round

8x1½ inches . . . . 1.2 L = 20x4 cm
9x1½ inches . . . . 1.5 L = 23x4 cm

Recipe Abbreviations

t. = teaspoon   ltr. = liter
T. = tablespoon   oz. = ounce
c. = cup   lb. = pound
pt. = pint   doz. = dozen
qt. = quart   pkg. = package
gal. = gallon   env. = envelope

Oven Temperatures

300° F . . . . 150° C
325° F . . . . 160° C
350° F . . . . 180° C
375° F . . . . 190° C
400° F . . . . 200° C
450° F . . . . 230° C

Kitchen Measurements

A pinch = ⅛ tablespoon
1 fluid ounce = 2 tablespoons
3 teaspoons = 1 tablespoon
4 fluid ounces = ½ cup
2 tablespoons = ⅛ cup
8 fluid ounces = 1 cup
4 tablespoons = ¼ cup
16 fluid ounces = 1 pint
8 tablespoons = ½ cup
32 fluid ounces = 1 quart
16 tablespoons = 1 cup
16 ounces net weight = 1 pound
2 cups = 1 pint
4 cups = 1 quart
4 quarts = 1 gallon